The Internet of Money V

The Internet of Money

Volume Two

A Collection of Talks by Andreas M. Antonopoulos

https://TheInternetOfMoney.org/

Dedicated to the bitcoin community

Disclaimers:

This book is edited commentary and opinion. Much of the content is based upon personal experience and anecdotal evidence. It is meant to promote thoughtful consideration of ideas, spur philosophical debate, and inspire further independent research. It is not investment advice; don't use it to make investment-related decisions. It's not legal advice; consult a lawyer in your jurisdiction with legal questions. It may contain errors and omissions, despite our best efforts. Andreas M. Antonopoulos, Merkle Bloom LLC, editors, copy editors, transcriptionists, and designers assume no responsibility for errors or omissions. Things change quickly in the bitcoin and blockchain industry; use this book as one reference, not your only reference.

References to trademarked or copyrighted works are for criticism and commentary only. Any trademarked terms are the property of their respective owners. References to individuals, companies, products, and services are included for illustration purposes only and should not be considered endorsements.

Licensing:

Almost all of Andreas's original work is distributed under creative commons licenses. Andreas has granted us CC-BY to modify and distribute the work included in this book in this way. If you would like to use portions of our book in your project, please send a request to licensing@merklebloom.com. We grant most license requests quickly and free of charge.

Talks by Andreas M. Antonopoulos

https://antonopoulos.com/

@aantonop

Cover Design

Kathrine Smith: http://kathrinevsmith.com/

Transcription and Editing

Jessica Levesque, Pamela Morgan, Janine Römer

Copyediting

Brooke Mallers, Ph.D.: @bitcoinmom

First print: **December 1, 2017**

Errata Submissions: errata@merklebloom.com

Licensing Requests: licensing@merklebloom.com

General: info@merklebloom.com

ISBN: 978-1-947910-06-5

Table of Contents

Preface

By Andreas M. Antonopoulos

When I started my journey in bitcoin, I never thought it would lead to this. This book is like an abridged diary of my discovery of bitcoin, delivered through a series of talks.

Over these past five years, I have delivered more than 170 talks to audiences across the world, recorded more than 200 podcast episodes, answered several hundred questions, participated in more than 150 interviews for radio, print and TV, appeared in eight documentaries and written a technical book called *Mastering Bitcoin* and I'm currently working on another technical book called *Mastering Ethereum*. Almost all of this work is available, for free, under open-source licenses, online. The talks included in this book are only a small sample of my work, selected by the editorial team to provide a glimpse into bitcoin, its uses, and its impact on the future.

Each of these talks was delivered to a live audience, without slides or any visual aides, and was mostly improvised. While I have a topic in mind before each talk, a lot of my inspiration comes from the energy and interaction with each audience. From talk to talk, the topics evolve as I try out new ideas, see the reaction and develop them further. Eventually, some ideas that start as a single sentence evolve, over several talks, into an entire topic.

This process of discovery is not perfect, of course. My talks are littered with minor factual errors. I recite dates, events, numbers, and technical details from memory and often get them wrong. In this book, my off-the-cuff errors, malapropisms, and verbal tics have been cleaned up by the editors. What remains is the essence of each presentation — how I wish it had been delivered, rather than a transcript of the actual delivery. But, with that cleanup there is also a price to pay. What is missing is the reaction and energy of the audience, the tone of my sentences, the spontaneous giggles from me and the people in the room. For all of that you have to watch the videos which are linked in Appendix C, *Video Links* of the book.

This book and my work over the past five years is about more than bitcoin. These talks reflect my worldview, my political ideas and my hopes, as well as my technical fascination and my unabashed geekiness. They summarize my enthusiasm about this technology and the astonishing future that I envision. This vision starts with bitcoin, a quirky cypherpunk experiment which unleashes a ripple of innovation, creating "The Internet of Money" and radically transforming society.

Note from the Editors

Almost the entire bitcoin community knows of Andreas's contribution to bitcoin. In addition to his written and audio work, he's a highly sought-after public speaker, lauded for consistently delivering innovative, thought-provoking, engaging talks. This book represents only a small sampling of Andreas's work in the bitcoin and blockchain industry over the past five years. With so much content, simply deciding what talks to include was an arduous task. We selected these specific talks because they fit the criteria of the book; we could easily have included dozens more. This book is Volume Two in The Internet of Money series, we hope to publish another volume soon.

We began this book project with a vision: to provide an easy-to-read, short-story style overview of why bitcoin matters, of why so many of us are excited about it. We wanted something we could share with family, friends, and co-workers that they might actually read: a compendium that they could pick up for five minutes, no-commitment, or explore for a few hours. It needed to be engaging, with real-world analogies to make the tech understandable. It needed to be inspirational, with a vision of how these things could positively impact humanity. It needed to be honest, acknowledging the shortcomings of our current systems and the technology itself.

Despite our best efforts, we're sure there are things we could improve and change. We've edited heavily in some places, for readability, while always trying to preserve the essence of the talk. We believe we've struck a good balance and we're pleased with the book as a whole. We hope you are too. If you've read Volume One, you'll notice some small changes in Volume Two. We've removed the large quoted sections; a big thank you to everyone who provided feedback. We've also included a question and answer section, highlighting some of the most commonly asked questions and Andreas's answers to them. If you have comments about editing, content, or suggestions about how we can make the book better, please email us at errata@merklebloom.com.

Tips to make your reading experience even better:

Each talk is intended to stand alone. There is no need to start at the beginning — although if you are unfamiliar with bitcoin, you may want to start at the first talk, "Introduction to Bitcoin," to get an overview of the topic.

You'll find a robust index at the end of the book. One of the things we're most proud of is the index. We've worked hard to provide an index that will allow you to cross-reference and research themes and topics.

Introduction to Bitcoin

Singularity University's IPP Conference; Silicon Valley, California; September 2016

Video Link: https://youtu.be/l1si5ZWLgy0

Nerd Money

Good morning, everyone! For a moment, forget everything you think you know about bitcoin, forget everything you've heard about blockchains, and let's start from basics.

In 2011, I heard about bitcoin for the first time, and my reaction was exactly the same as almost everybody else who heard about bitcoin for the first time: "Ha! Nerd money. That's probably just for gambling." Six months later, I heard about bitcoin again, and this time I read the white paper that launched this system. My background in computer science and distributed systems allowed me to see behind the illusion of what I thought bitcoin was, and it blew my mind.

My Sixth Obsession

In my life, I have now had six occasions in which I have become absolutely obsessed with a system of technology, to the point of forgetting to eat, forgetting to sleep, and shamelessly consuming as much knowledge as possible: my first computer when I was 10 years old; my first programming language experience; my first modem; my first access to the web via a web browser; the first time I downloaded and installed the Linux operating system; and now bitcoin.

During the first four months after I discovered bitcoin, I lost 26 pounds on the highly inadvisable diet of obsession. I have not completely emerged from that obsession, because I keep finding new layers of depth to understand. The reason bitcoin is so fascinating is because it isn't what it appears to be at first glance.

Bitcoin Is the Sixth Innovation in Money

Bitcoin isn't money; it isn't a system of currency. It's not a company, it's not a product, it's not a service you sign up for. It's not a currency; currency is just the first application. It is the concept of decentralization applied to the human communication of value. It is a platform of trust.

What *is* money? As INQ (the artist who performed just before Andreas) said, it's an illusion, it's imaginary. The reason we don't grasp that is because it's so deeply embedded in our civilization.

Money is one of the oldest technologies that humanity has. It precedes writing. How do we know that? The very first samples of writing we have are tallies and ledgers of debts owed. We could speculate that money had an oral tradition until it needed to invent a written tradition, so writing was created for it.

In the history of money that now spans tens of thousands of years, there have been maybe five major changes. From pure barter exchange to the introduction of the first abstraction of value—shells, feathers, beads, nuts, stones. Then precious metals, and then paper money, and then plastic money. And now network money. Bitcoin introduces a platform on which you can run currency as an application, on a network without any central points of control, a system completely decentralized like the internet itself. It is not money for the internet, but rather the *Internet of Money*.

Money is a Language

Again, what is money? Money is a language, a linguistic abstraction. Money is a language that we use to communicate value to each other. Money simply allows us to express value, and that value may have economic consequences, but it also has other consequences. We use money to express and create social bonds, relationships, and associations—to create organization.

Bitcoin is the first system of money that is not controlled by any entity, that is completely decentralized. Bitcoin introduces to money the very same things that the internet brought to communication. If money is speech, if money is a language, and you disconnect it from all other media and you make it pure speech, pure content, an internet content-type, a protocol designation, money over IP—then the concept of money can be separated from the previous notions of nations as sovereign issuers, of institutions that wield control.

We move from institution-based money to network-based money.

Of course, everyone will welcome this move with open arms, right? Not a chance. What do you think they said the first time someone was presented with a gold depository certificate instead of a gold coin? They said, "Uhh, that's not money! Go away." What do you think happened in 1950 the first time someone showed up at a motel, presented their Diner's Club membership card, and said, "I'll pay with this piece of plastic"? They said, "That's not money! Go away."

Programmable Money, Exponential Innovation

Now, we're on the verge of a new transformation of money. We're creating the first completely global, completely borderless, completely decentralized, and completely open form of money. Because this money is programmable, you can build applications. You can launch and run your applications on the bitcoin network without asking anyone for permission. Just like you can launch a website without permission on the internet. The only requirement to have a successful application on the Internet of Money is two interested participants—that is your market segment.

What happens when you remove the requirement for permission? When you push innovation to the edge of the network? An exponential explosion in innovation. Applications that could not be built on the old systems—because they required permission, because they required a significantly large market segment, because they required adoption by many in order to be available at all—now, none of those requirements exist. Anyone in the world can write or download an application—or even use a feature phone with text messaging—and immediately acquire the same powers that institutions of banking have today.

Personhood Is No Longer Required

When I say "anyone," that's only scratching the surface because, ironically enough, not only does programmable money not recognize borders, it also does not recognize people. It doesn't matter if you're a person or a refrigerator or a self-driving car. Throughout the history of money, ownership of currency required personhood, either as an individual or as an association of individuals in a corporation. Bitcoin can be owned by machines, bitcoin can be owned by software agents; machines can pay each other and those payments are not just about economic activity. They are the basis for market-based security systems, the basis for creating bonds of authentication between devices, the basis of new applications that have never been done before.

A Unified System of Money

Bitcoin unifies systems of money. Today we have systems of money for small payments, systems of money for large payments. We have systems of money for payments between individuals, for payments between companies, and for payments between governments.

Does that remind you of something? That's how communication used to be before the internet. We had systems of communication for pictures, systems of communications for letters, systems of communication for short-distance and long-distance. The internet came along and unified all of those. The Internet of Money creates a single network which can handle everything from a microtransaction to a gigatransaction—in seconds, anywhere in the world, for any participant, without permission.

Constructing New Languages

But if you only look at the application of money, you're missing the point, because you can take the language, the building blocks of this platform, and use them to construct other languages that communicate value: tokens, reward points, brand-loyalty coins.

Today, there are over a thousand digital currencies using the design pattern, the recipe, of bitcoin. Most of them are junk, some of them are not. Over the next decade, we are going to see tens of thousands and then hundreds of thousands of coins. Some will have economic use, some will simply be expressions of loyalty or affiliation. These digital coins or tokens will represent items in the physical world: the title for a house, for example; or the controlling key for a car that can be transferred from one owner to another, and five seconds later that owner can step into the car and drive away, because the car can validate the new ownership. We cannot yet imagine what other applications we're going to build around this platform of trust.

Money-Mediated Social Relationships (Social Constructs)

Money arises spontaneously from the social constructs of homo sapiens. It even arises in primates. You can teach monkeys money, and they will learn how to exchange abstract tokens for food and then use them to build social relationships. They'll also invent strong-arm robbery: they'll beat up another monkey, take away its pebbles, eat the bananas.

Children invent money. In kindergarten they use blocks, rubber bands, Pokémon cards, and other little tokens—abstractions of value that they exchange to strengthen social bonds, to express loyalty and friendship, to learn about sharing. In the near future, children will be building currencies, only this time these currencies will be global, unforgeable, and scalable on day one. A few years from now, Maria will be launching "MariaCoin" in her kindergarten to compete against "JoeyCoin." It won't really matter to anyone, until of course Justin Bieber launches "JustinBieberCoin" and it happens to surpass the market capitalization of thirty nations on this planet, and we are all writing horrified opinion editorials about how the world is going to hell.

Banking Has Changed Forever

What's happening with this technology is astonishingly deep. Certainly, for some of the companies in this room, it's a bit scary. Banking has never been the most innovative sector in the world because there is a very careful balance between innovation and the conservative fiduciary duty that exists in banking—that *must* exist—when you control other people's money. **Yet, with bitcoin, you don't control other people's money.** In bitcoin, *I* control my money. I have complete and total authority over my bitcoin; it cannot be seized, it cannot be frozen, it cannot be censored. My transactions cannot be intercepted and they cannot be stopped. I can transact with almost complete anonymity, and so can anyone just five minutes after they download an application.

The idea that you can proceed in the industry of money, in the industries of commerce, and maintain the same conservative attitude that has existed for centuries, ever since merchants in Venice and Amsterdam started issuing depository certificates and providing banking services-- is gone. You cannot operate closed systems that have borders and require permission to join, at a rate of innovation controlled by the most conservative tendencies within your organization, because now you are competing with a technology that enables exponential growth, exponential innovation at the edges—without permission—by anyone in the world.

Banking the Unbanked, Debanking All of Us

Today this technology is serving the privileged elite. If you can open a brokerage account online and be trading on the Tokyo stock market within 12 hours in yen, you are among the elite-- only one-and-a-half billion people have that privilege. But this technology is not about the elite. It's about everyone else. Of the other 6 billion people on this planet, 4 billion are significantly underbanked, and an astonishing 2 billion people are completely unbanked. They will leapfrog; they will never have a relationship with a bank and they're not the only ones.

Children born today will never have a bank account. They will have a bank _app_—not a bank app that gives them access to their bank account, but a bank app that makes them a banker, an international banker in an app. They will not be permitted to open a traditional bank account until they are 16 years old; by that time, I hope they will have at least six or more years of experience with digital currencies. I would like to watch them walk into a bank branch to have someone explain to them what "three to five business days" means.

Children born today will likely never get a driving license because there will be self-driving cars. They will also never use paper money, because by the time they get to an age when they really start using adult money, there will be no paper money. It will seem as anachronistic as a fax machine or a horse and buggy seems to us.

Exponential Innovation from a Complex Recipe

Giving access to billions of people is exponential innovation, on a global basis. They have enormous need and this system offers them a solution. But the system is not ready yet: it's nascent, complex, and impossible to use for most people.

In 1989, I sent my first email. In order to do so, I had to compile a version of the Unix mail program using a C compiler and Unix command-line skills. I had to set it up on the command line, type out my email, and that email was then transmitted across the great internet in an astonishing *three* days. 20 years later, my mother replicated that experience with a swipe of her finger on her iPad.

Bitcoin today, and all of the currencies that are built using that recipe, are at the same stage that the internet was in 1992. Only now we have the internet, and so the rate of exponential growth has already started. The innovation is growing at an astonishing rate. I spend every single day, full-time, trying to keep up with bitcoin and it's almost impossible.

The Gift of Financial Autonomy

Do not underestimate this. Do not listen to the people who tell you that bitcoin is just for pornographers, terrorists, drug dealers, and gamblers. Remember that they said the exact same thing about the internet. But when 2 or 3 million people got online, we found out that they are not interested in those things—they are interested in sharing cat videos, and now we have an internet of a billion cat videos.

When you take digital currency mainstream and give it to the 4 billion people who have been isolated from international finance and commerce—and you give them the opportunity to control their money against despotic governments and corrupt banks that are stealing from them—you give them the opportunity to control their future. You give them the opportunity to transact with everyone in the world, to own title to their own property in a fully transferable digital token that is recognized everywhere. You give them control over finance that cannot be seized, frozen, or censored. They will buy food, healthcare, sanitation, education, shelter—because that's what people do.

The underbanked and unbanked will not be denied this technology. **The Internet of Money was launched on January 3rd, 2009. This language, this currency, this wave of innovation is coming.** It's coming faster than you can imagine. It's deeper than you can fathom. It's more sophisticated than you can immediately understand. It takes years of study just to see all of the implications.

It is a gift to the entire world, a technology that represents the sixth greatest innovation in the technology of money, the most ancient technology of our civilization.

Thank you.

Blockchain vs. Bullshit

Blockchain Africa Conference at Focus Rooms; Johannesburg, South Africa; March 2017

Video Link: https://youtu.be/SMEOKDVXlUo

Greatest Tech or Biggest Hype?

A couple of years ago this conference was called the "Bitcoin Conference"; now it's the "Blockchain Conference." Next year, it's probably going to be the "DLT Technology Conference," and then after that it'll be the "Database-Inspircd-by-but-No-Longer-in-Any-Way-Related-to-Blockchain Conference." It's an interesting progression and, as you'll see, relevant to our discussion today.

So, let's get started. What exactly is going on here? Is this the greatest technological innovation and explosion of innovation since the mobile internet? Maybe even since the internet itself? Or is this the greatest load of hype ever arranged around a technology in the history of technology? Both, and in fact that's a characteristic of advanced technologies.

I often say that where bitcoin and the other open blockchains are today is approximately where the internet was in 1992—in terms of technology, in terms of infrastructure deployment, in terms of adoption patterns. But while this technology is approximately where the internet was in 1992, the *hype* around "blockchain" is exactly where the hype around the internet was in 1998. And you know what comes next. There will be a shakeout.

When the waters recede, you'll see who on the beach wasn't wearing a swimsuit. They'll stand there naked. This will happen in the blockchain space. There is *a lot* of bullshit being peddled to venture capitalists, to investors, to initial-coin-offering or ICO buyers, to uneducated investors. There are a lot of Ponzi schemes and pyramid schemes. There are a lot of empty promises. There is also a lot of business as usual disguised as innovation, disguised as disruptive technology.

Security Awareness and Applied Cryptography

We're at this strange moment when the underlying technology truly is massively disruptive, massively innovative. The amount of research that's happening today in applied cryptography is unprecedented. **We are looking at the largest civilian deployment of public key cryptography ever, because it turns out that people only protect keys when those keys are attached to value.** Nothing teaches someone about security faster than having their bitcoin on a Windows machine.

Owning bitcoin quickly changes your attitude towards information security. Before bitcoin, you didn't care about securing your photos; some didn't even care about the sexy photos! You didn't care about your location, the fact that everything you did was tracked. You didn't care about posting your entire life on Facebook. You used the same password, "password1234," on 17 different sites. You didn't know what two-factor authentication was.

Then, bitcoin happened. Suddenly you're on a steep learning curve and getting better every day. Now you're telling your friends about two-factor authentication and you're horrified to remember how you used to practice security. Storing value has this unique ability to focus your mind on the aspects of security that matter.

This technology is driving this groundswell of security awareness. It's driving the most incredible research in applied cryptography we've ever seen. Some of you are probably quite technical; you're involved in computer science, you've seen what's happening here. Nobody thought that we would be doing applied Schnorr signatures. Nobody thought we'd be looking at advanced elliptic-curve applications. Nobody thought we'd be doing things like ring signatures and range proofs for Confidential Transactions. The state of anonymity and privacy is advancing rapidly. We're building a whole new world in terms of cryptography, and this is applied cryptography on the largest cryptographically-secured network the world has ever seen.

This is not business as usual. It's highly disruptive.

Blockchain Is NOT the Technology Behind Bitcoin

Out of the hype arose this fantastic saying, "Blockchain is the technology behind bitcoin," which is incorrect. **Blockchain is one of the four foundational technologies (Blockchain, Proof-of-Work, P2P Network, and Cryptography) behind bitcoin, and it can't stand alone.** But that hasn't stopped people from trying to sell it.

Today, "blockchain" is bitcoin with a haircut and suit that you parade in front of your board. It's the ability to deliver a sanitized, clean, comfortable version of bitcoin, to people who are too terrified of truly disruptive technology. You enter this very strange world, where the words no longer mean anything.

Can you define "blockchain"? I think a few people in this room could probably define "blockchain." The real challenge would be: can you define "blockchain" in such a way that I can't do search-and-replace with the word "database" and still make that sentence work? Because that's the challenge: if what you're doing is a database with signatures, it's not interesting. It's boring.

The Essence of Bitcoin: Revolutionizing Trust

What is the essence of bitcoin? It's not blockchain. **The essence of bitcoin is the ability to operate in a decentralized way without having to trust anyone.** The essence of bitcoin is to be able to use software to authoritatively and independently verify everything yourself—without appeal to authority.

In bitcoin, you don't trust the other nodes you're talking to. You assume they're lying. You don't trust the miners. You don't trust the people creating the transactions. You don't trust anything other than the outcome of your own verification and validation. Through that, you end up trusting in something more important: the network effect.

Decentralized Security Through Computation

Bitcoin introduced the concept of decentralized security through computation, and this has not yet sunk in. Bitcoin represents a new security model. It replaces the security model based around concentric circles of access and control with an institution in the center, with a security model that is inside-out, open, and accessible to everyone. This security model is based on market forces and game theory. **It is the first market-based security model**, in which a series of incentives and punishments ensures what the ultimate result is: you can trust the platform itself, as a neutral arbiter that is not controlled by anyone, without third parties, without intermediaries.

Bitcoin revolutionizes *trust*.

Open Blockchains

I use the qualifier "open" to talk about *open blockchains*, meaning the applications of this technology that enable you to run a decentralized, trustless system that does not rely on anyone as an intermediary of trust. Because *that* is the disruption here. *That* is the essence of this technology.

That essence is present in some other systems besides bitcoin. For example, Ethereum exhibits it for the application of smart contracts. But those smart contracts only work if you don't have to trust anyone to execute the smart contract correctly and that depends on everyone being able to participate in an open manner, verifying information independently, and everyone having access to the underlying consensus algorithm.

Characteristics of Trust Networks

Out of these characteristics comes the power of these blockchain technologies:

Open. That's the key word.

Borderless. There are no borders.

Transnational. This is no longer about nation-states; this is about network-centric trust. Without third parties, the network *is* the trusted party but only if you verify everything.

Neutral. It isn't serving the goals of any one organization or institution. It follows the consensus rules neutrally; everyone follows the consensus rules neutrally. There is no such thing as a "good" transaction or a "bad" transaction, a "valuable" transaction or a "spam" transaction, an "authorized" transaction or an "unauthorized" transaction, a "legal" transaction or an "illegal" transaction. In these systems, there is only a *valid* or an *invalid* transaction, based on the consensus rules. It doesn't matter who the sender is, who the recipient is, or what the value or asset or smart contract that's being executed is . Neutrality, radical neutrality.

Censorship resistance. In order for the system to be open, borderless, transnational, and neutral, it must be able to defend these properties by making it impossible for any actor—or even several colluding actors—to censor, disrupt, blacklist, restrict, seize, or freeze transactions, or prevent users or countries from participating in this network.

Those are the important characteristics of these new, open, decentralized systems of trust that do not depend on institutions.

Is It Blockchain or Bullshit?

What I'd like to equip you with is a set of criteria to understand when you are being presented with something—perhaps to invest in, or to be employed by, or to engage in some way—that calls itself a "blockchain," a "distributed ledger," or one of these other names that are coming out. How can you tell—blockchain or bullshit?

They both start with a *b*, but what's the difference?

- If you can replace the word "blockchain" with "database" and the brochure reads the same, it's business as usual.

- If it's not decentralized, borderless, neutral, censorship-resistant, or open, then it's not innovating.

- If it re-establishes trust in intermediaries, it's just a database, and that is not disruptive.

The idea that we're going to take this technology and use it to improve the operating margins of centralized institutions of trust so that they can continue business as usual? I'd say it's abhorrent, but that's a strong word. It's just boring—really, really boring. No one got into this in order to make a few billion for a financial-services clearing house. If you did, I'm really sorry, but that's boring.

What's really exciting is the possibility of fundamentally changing the way we allocate trust on this planet—opening up the ability to collaborate, transact, and engage on a global level with everyone.

Simply by downloading an application, you can become part of a giant platform of trust that doesn't care who you are or where you came from, that doesn't require permission to participate or innovate. Where a 12-year-old JavaScript programmer has the same influence and power as JPMorgan Chase—more, in fact, because the 12-year-old is doing open source and feeding into a community of collaboration that is creating a tsunami of innovation.

Permissioned "Distributed Ledgers"

Taking this technology and using it to strengthen the same centralized institutions so that they can improve their bottom line, is boring. That is not what blockchain is; that's just a database. It doesn't change anything. In fact, there are some rather disturbing possibilities in this model.

How DLTs Actually Work

Let's think about this for a second. The most commonly expressed application for these new "distributed ledger technologies," or *DLTs*, is to replace the function of a centralized clearing house with a consortium of n participants, where n is 2, 3, 4, 5, 10 known, permissioned, controlled participants, who will assemble transactions and sign them—rather than compete through market forces in a security model like bitcoin's.

They discard currency as the underlying mechanism for building market-based security. They discard proof-of-work as "wasteful," because all it allows you to do is a decentralized, secure, neutral, censorship-resistant blockchain. They discard the openness and trust five named parties to sign transactions according to rules the parties design.

At that point, they don't need to assemble these transactions in blocks. They can just sign the individual transactions; they don't need to chain them together because, absent proof-of-work and a system of currency incentives, rewriting that is easy. There's no immutability. It's not a blockchain anymore, because there are no blocks and there is no chain.

Now that's at a technical level, but let's look at the more important level: what happens when you replace a clearing house with a consortium of interested players?

Trusting the Cartel

Clearing houses, that validate exchanges between banks, provide value beyond clearing transactions. One of the most important features of a clearing house is that it is *not* a participant in the market; it has no skin in the game. The New York Stock Exchange is not an active trader. That's not an accident; that's called *separation of concerns*. The clearing house is an independent party with oversight and is not a market participant. If you remove the independent party replace it with five banks, all of which have skin in the game, how do you ensure integrity when the incentives to cheat, front-run, manipulate the market, and break the consensus rules—even adversarially against the other four parties—are so high? There's no incentive to keep the consensus rules. Essentially they're saying, "Trust us, we're in a consortium."

"Trust us"? These five banks? Where were you in 2008? Where were you when LIBOR was fixed? Where were you when the gold markets were fixed? Where were you when front-running and high-frequency trading were creating these monsters of crony capitalism? "Trust us"? Hell no!

Removing the clearing house and replacing it with... what's the word?... it's not *consortium*_... *Oh yes, _cartel*, that's the word! Replacing it with a cartel of the *same* market makers who have manipulated and compromised every market in history, and doing that in a way that shields them from transparency. That's not a recipe for efficiency, immutability, security, or transparency. **That's not a blockchain, that's bullshit—very profitable bullshit.** It requires you to have confidence in the game. A con game, as it's known.

Be careful. When you see these technologies—whose fundamental purpose is to remove trusted intermediaries and create an open, borderless, neutral system— being turned into a tool for a bunch of untrustworthy "trusted parties" to manipulate markets, there is going to be a disaster. And they're going to do it.

I have some consolation in the fact that their keys will leak. When you centralize a system, you have to have perfect security. None of them has ever managed to do that. All of the companies involved in this brave new business-as-usual space have been hacked, breached, leaked, whistle-blown a dozen times. They can't keep information secure, no one can! **The whole point of a decentralized blockchain is that you don't keep the information secure; you spread it out so thin there's no place to attack it directly. That's what makes it secure.**

What happens when you concentrate it among five participants? I can't wait for the Anonymous-WikiLeaks collaborative dump of the titans of Wall Street and their ledger of every transaction they've ever done. I can't wait, it's going to be so much fun. And it *is* going to happen.

The Real Opportunities

People are examining this market; they're grasping and reaching out in darkness. When you have a brand new disruptive technology, you can't see the margins. It's like stumbling around in a dark room. Somewhere in there is a billion-dollar company; somewhere in there is an opportunity. You have to figure out what market exists that will create opportunity, that will change the world, that will have an impact on humanity.

Entrepreneurs look at other people's problems and see them as opportunities. When journalists in 1997 were writing about "the imminent failure of the internet" because of the impossibility of finding anything, Larry Page and Sergey Brin were finding stuff and building a multi-billion-dollar empire on solving the unsolvable problem of search.

There are seemingly unsolvable problems in the open, decentralized, public, transparent, neutral, censorship-resistant, global, trustless network platform that is the blockchain. These blockchains—bitcoin, Ethereum, and the many other open systems—are gradually trying to find their niche.

The Three Elements to Success

Where are those markets? There are three elements to success in this industry. The first one is identifying a viable market. You've got to stumble in the dark and find something useful. Very often, the people stumbling in the dark don't find anything useful. In 1998, Pets.com was building an online-commerce empire for pet supplies. It was too early. The market didn't exist.

Before Peapod, the web grocer Webvan was delivering groceries to homes in San Francisco. It failed miserably. Was that the right market? Maybe, but it was the wrong time. That's the second important element: the right timing. You can identify something that, at some point, will be enormous, but you're off by a decade.

Then the most important factor: sequencing. The prerequisite. Why did Facebook not happen in 1992? We didn't have enough density of adoption. We didn't have mobile devices that were permanently connected. We didn't even have home-based internet that was permanently on. We didn't have a dense social network in order to engage with the people you knew, because the people we knew barely had email or didn't have email. You can't build a system of complexity that depends on many-to-many interaction with high density when the market is still focused on delivering applications that are one-to-one with low density.

To use an example from science, it's like trying to fuse hydrogen directly into carbon. You can't do that. You've got helium, lithium, beryllium but you've got a long way to go and you need to keep smashing things together before you get enough density to start doing interesting things like organic chemistry.

The bottom line is you can't do advanced real-estate title applications, voting on the blockchain, retail markets at scale.   You can't do consumer-to-consumer dense markets. You can't do point-of-sale retail with these systems. *Yet.* You can't do many of the things yet that might be very interesting markets. The reason you can't do them is because there's not enough liquidity, there aren't enough users, there is not enough adoption. The user interfaces are terrible, the applications are still at their infant stage. That doesn't mean these things *can't* happen. It just means they're not happening this year.

Maturing out of Infancy

In order for people to have the trust to put the title of their home on this blockchain, it has to be able to secure not billions but *trillions of dollars* in assets. In order to be able to secure trillions of dollars in assets, it has to have liquidity and infrastructure. It has to have broad adoption. You're not going to get adoption on a transaction that most people do twice in their lifetime, when you can't even get them to use it for transactions they do every day.

Mass adoption takes time. For the first 15 years of the internet, the application was email; not until everybody had it, had to have it, and needed it for work, did we see the second layer emerge because that created the density of adoption.

Currency is the email of blockchains. Payments are the fundamental infrastructure that will enable density of adoption. It's very, very enticing to say, "This is about more than money!" It absolutely is, in the long term. The vision of this technology is far beyond money, but you can't build that unless you first build the money part. That's what creates the security. That's what creates the velocity, the liquidity, the infrastructure. That's what funds the entire ecosystem.

In the end, when we do deliver these services to people, it won't be so they can open a bank account. **This isn't about banking the unbanked; it's about unbanking all of us.**

Thank you.

Fake News, Fake Money

Silicon Valley Bitcoin Meetup at Plug and Play Tech Center; Sunnyvale, California; April 2017

Video Link: https://youtu.be/i_wOEL6dprg

The Purveyors of Fake News

"Fake news" has been in the news a lot lately. We have all of these accusations swirling around. The established media—the *New York Times*, the _Washington Post_—are pointing fingers at "these purveyors of fake news," primarily internet-based sites. And internet-based sites are pointing right back and saying, "Do you remember Judith Miller? 'There are WMDs with aluminum tubes in Iraq!' Bullshit." Fake news happens on both sides.

We see well-established backbones of authority and truth, like the *New York Times* and the *Washington Post*, or even CNN, Fox News and other TV channels like CBS and ABC, cheerleading for a war based on false premises—and that was just last week, again! Not Iraq, but Syria this time. Have we learned? No, we haven't learn anything.

How did we arrive here, in a world where we can't even tell what's true and what isn't? Why do we have this debate over fake news? Part of it has to do with the rise of the internet in the early 90s.

The Death of Fact Checking

The internet didn't disrupt newspapers and television companies by stealing their audience for news; that came much, much later. First, the internet disrupted their most profitable revenue sources. For newspapers, that was the classified-advertising section. That was where they made most of their money, in small-business advertising and the classified section. The internet came along and Craigslisted all of it, just completely undermined it. Now you can do all of it for free, and it's instantaneous. Boom! Suddenly, the source of their most profitable revenue disappears and the newspapers have to adapt.

Then, it happened again with television. They started losing advertising revenue to the new popular websites that were getting more eyeballs. First, they started losing the local and small advertisers, who were now able to position ads and target specific demographics and audiences, because they could get much more fine-grained information. Television is a one-way thing; you have no idea who is watching. With targeted advertising on the internet, television started losing revenue, too.

So, what did they do? They trimmed the fat. "Journalists? We don't really need them. No foreign desk, cut that. Investigative journalism? Cut that. What's selling more papers? 'Ask Judy,' the astrology section, infotainment, cartoons, and sensationalist news. If it bleeds, it leads."

Inexorably, the long downtrend of the news industry started. They gutted their foreign desks, they gutted their investigative journalism, they gutted their fact checking, they gutted their copyeditor desks. What was left was a bunch of interns, running around copying the press releases of powerful corporations and presenting them as fact, taking notes when someone who was seemingly important said something, not questioning any of it, just writing it down and publishing it—as truth.

Citations and Sources of Truth

"Fake news" has happened because the basis for producing truth has been removed from the very institutions whose job it was to produce truth. This has caused a weird situation because, prior to the "fake news" era, how did you know if something was true? Well, the *New York Times* said it, the *Washington Post* said it, it was on CBS. Surely, they have fact checked it, therefore it must be the truth.

The fundamental basis for discovery of truth has been to appeal to the source. If you were writing an essay in a college course, your professor would ask, "What are you basing this argument on? Give me citations. Source your argument. Where are the facts?" If you took a headline from the *New York Times* and sourced it, they'd say, "Okay, great. That's a citation from a valid source."

We used the *issuer* to determine the quality of what they issued. We looked at the authority of the news based on the authority of the *institution* that said it. Because that *was* a good model, a good heuristic. It gave us a good false-positive, false-negative ratio. It was a bet. It was a way to say, "I can't fact check all of that, but these people have. If I read, I will become not only educated but also informed."

However, we're now in the situation where the people who watch the most TV and read the most newspapers are the *least* informed part of the electorate. How did that happen? The institutions are still standing. Their authority is still standing in some eyes. The basis of credibility is still there. They still have the big buildings and wide circulation and big names. But the mechanism that delivered truth is no longer there. The mechanism that ensured quality is no longer there, or is significantly eroded.

What's their response to that? "We'll try harder"? No. They turn to the internet and say, "You're fake news!"

Arguably, a lot of the stuff on the internet *is* fake news, because it never had any of these mechanisms for producing truth. But the internet that never had the mechanisms, and the newspapers that no longer have the mechanisms, are now producing truth on a relatively equal basis. Every now and then, some blogger uncovers some incredible story that nobody's noticed. And it is the truth and the networks pick it up. Every now and then, the institutions of traditional truth fall flat on their faces and deliver bullshit to us, packaged in a fancy name.

The result is that people start questioning whether they should believe anything.

The Mechanisms of Truth Discovery

What's the option? Where do we go from here? Do we have to evaluate every fact for ourselves? Do we have to build into our critical thinking the fact-checking department that they fired? How do we go about evaluating every piece of knowledge as fact or fake news?

Well, there's an *easy* heuristic. If the esteemed leader of your political party says it's fake news, then it's fake news. Now, we outsource fact finding to the tribe that we belong to. If the tribal leader says that those guys are lying, we just go with it. Happens in bitcoin, too. Tribalism is part of human nature. What's really interesting is that what just happened in news—that has left an entire generation of people now unable to discern truth from fiction and easily manipulated through propaganda— I'm about to suggest today that this is about to happen to money.

Illusions of Value

How do you know money is valuable? I get asked this question every time I do a seminar about bitcoin, usually from someone new to bitcoin. They say, "But bitcoin isn't backed by anything. This thing I have in my pocket, it says *Central Bank of Blah Blah*. It's backed by the nation / queen / king / parliament / GDP of my country or the gold that we have in our vaults."

You don't have any gold in your vaults! Many people still think there's gold in the vaults. It's a common misconception. Most of our understanding of money comes from myth. It is just barely removed from the level of myth that is Santa Claus. We have this constructed fantasy about money, that we received as children. As adults, when we notice inconsistencies, we just shore it up with some rusty nails and planks to keep it in place. **We try to keep the illusion. As part of that, we adopt these preposterous ideas such as "there's gold in the vaults."**

Losing Faith

We had a heuristic. The heuristic was: if a stable democratic government, based on some broadly free principles, sanely manages the economy and says the money has value, then it has value. That's a great heuristic. That removes the necessity for us to independently evaluate every note that comes into our hands. Will this still be worth $20 tomorrow? Okay, not this one because it was counterfeit, but this other "real" one? Yeah, it will be worth $20. Maybe it won't buy you $20 worth in today's money; maybe it will buy you $19.80 worth in a year. You don't really notice that, it's okay. You trust that it's still going to be there.

Unless you're Greek. Or Cypriot. Or Venezuelan. Or Argentinian. Or Brazilian. Or Zimbabwean. Or from the Ukraine. Just keep adding to that list; it's happened so many times. One day, you wake up and you discover the banks are closed. The bank governor is on TV saying, "People, don't panic! Everything is under control!" When a government official says that, you know: that's the time to panic. Now it's about who gets to line up in front of the bank, because they're not opening next week as they promised. The temporary emergency measure will become a permanent emergency measure. Guaranteed, every time. So line up and run for your money in the bank.

Suddenly, the institution of money has crumbled. Now what do you trust? You go back to basics, things you can examine and validate for yourself: gold, chicken, rice, salt, sugar, whatever you can get your hands on. Or that other country's money. The U.S. dollar is hard currency, right?

Full Faith and Credit Requires Reciprocity

The concept of money is one of those things that holds value primarily because we attribute the value as a direct result of its issuance by a trusted authority. We outsource our own determination of value to this trusted third party. What happens when that trusted third party stops delivering on that promise? On purpose? By accident? Through mismanagement? Who knows? what happens when the phrase that seemed so meaningful, strong, and satisfying—"the full faith and credit of the U.S.government"—loses meaning, strength, and satisfaction.

"The *full* faith," not just *some* of the faith! The full faith and credit of the entire United States of America! They give you their full faith and credit, and in return you give them all of *your* full faith and credit. Compare that to this one: "The full faith and credit of the national bank of Zimbabwe." That phrase no longer has much weight to it, that phrase that you put all your faith in.

Every time you receive one of those bills, you are giving credit—you are giving them a product or a service in return for the bill, that's credit. You are giving faith. **Your full faith and credit is based on absolutely no rational thinking, other than you somehow believe in the phrase "the full faith and credit."**

I have a prediction. This phrase is going to become increasingly untenable—not just in the hotspots, not just in the backwaters, not just in the developing nations and the "third worlds," as we used to call them, but in many places simultaneously. $220 trillion of debt says that "the full faith and credit" is ringing hollow all around the world. What happens when they can no longer shore it up?

Exiting the System

Bitcoin is not trying to become a national currency. Oh no, it's doing something far more dangerous. It's encouraging people to put their savings outside the system. That is the worst thing you can do to a system based on full faith and credit. We're taking away the credit and the faith, by presenting an alternative that some people will find more useful. In some places, where the full faith and credit of the national currency has been damaged, they will flock to bitcoin as a valuable alternative, because they know that it's safer.

We're seeing that happen. We saw it happen en masse after November 8th in India, when the Indian government demonetized 86 percent of the country's money. Where's the faith now? No full faith. Can you print on the money "14 percent of the faith and credit of the National Bank of India"? We took out 86 percent, so that leaves 14 percent. The statement, "This money is backed by 14 percent of the full faith and credit of the National Bank of India," doesn't sound so good. People flocked to bitcoin.

Similarly, it wasn't bloggers challenging the truth of news that created this dichotomy of fake news; it wasn't better news gathering that undermined the newspapers. It was the process of undermining their advertising revenue, cutting off their feed, cutting them off at the knees, and then forcing them to adjust their news gathering to the new level of income they had.

What happens when bitcoin does that to banks? Because when they say, "Close all the doors and keep all the money in," there's one door they can't close: it's bitcoin. The money keeps leaking and leaking. So, they put the minister on television and have him tell everyone that everything's going to be fine: "The yuan will not be devalued any further. The full faith and credit of the People's Bank of China is behind this currency." Then a month later, it's devalued another half percent. That has happened many times in the past year. At some point, the people say to themselves, *That statement doesn't count any more. I'm taking my money elsewhere.* A few people do. A trickle of billions of dollars has fled into bitcoin from the yuan.

Bitcoin is not offering a better way for people to buy things, to invest in companies, to transact with each other; the damage is much more insidious. Bitcoin is undercutting the very source of revenue, value, and stability of a national currency by removing "the full faith and credit" of the people and putting it into an alternative currency. People are taking their savings and, instead of putting it into a deposit account where it becomes the basis for fractional-reserve lending, they're sucking the liquidity out of the economy, and that's the worst thing you can do with an economy like that.

The "Fake Money!" Hysteria

So, what are they doing next? What can do they now? Drag the finance minister on TV to say, "Dear citizens: Drug dealers, terrorists, pornographers, criminals, and most importantly, those really nasty people who live in the country next door—they are undermining our nation through this fake currency, bitcoin, the fake money! They are in a criminal conspiracy to damage our economy! Don't trust it. Do not invest your money in this bitcoin. It's fake money. It's backed by nothing!" "Fake money! Fake money! Fake money!" they cry and scream and protest.

You think that's not happening? It's happening right now. Watch, or translate if you like, what the Venezuelans said about bitcoin just a few months ago. "Fake money!" In fact, they said, "It's the Colombians doing it!" It's always the weirdos next door who speak with a funny accent and prefer soft tacos instead of hard tacos. Abomination! And so the cry starts, slowly at first: "Fake money, fake money, fake money!" Bitcoin is considered fake money in a few places in the world. Where do you think it's considered fake money? Not here. Nobody's called bitcoin "fake money" here. Certainly no official would do that; they would rather it remain in obscurity. But in Venezuela, bitcoin is "fake money." In Zimbabwe, bitcoin is "fake money." In China, they've tried the "fake money" narrative a few times; it hasn't played very well with the audience.

When in Doubt, Ask the Market

In the absence of institutional authority, there is no basis for evaluating whether money is real or not. Or is there? What is fake money and real money? Who knows? Are we back in the same conundrum? Are we back in the same situation, where we can no longer tell the difference? Is this just like fake news? Do we all have to discover the truth for ourselves? No, because money has markets and markets discover truth. That's what markets do.

If you want to know if bitcoin is fake money, or if the bolivar is fake money, you have an easy test. Take bitcoin and bolivar to someone on the street and ask, "How much will you give me for each of these?" **If the official exchange rate for the bolivar is five times less than the unofficial exchange rate, and if the official exchange rate for bitcoin carries a 20 percent premium, the market is telling you exactly which money is fake.**

The market discovers truth. No matter how many pronouncements, currency controls, bank bans, bank holidays, and demonetization incidents you attempt. No matter how big you try to make that wall or how strong you try to make that dam, with a little pin prick the water starts flowing through, and once it's got a little flow, that hole gets bigger, and there's no stopping it. The truth will come out. The truth will be evaluated by the market. You can call bitcoin "fake money" and the market will say, "Well, I'd rather take that fake money than your fake money."

Bitcoin Market Valuation

On November 8th in India, the price of bitcoin went up and maintained a 22 percent premium against the rupee over any other currency in the world. When I went to India I was asked, "Why is bitcoin so expensive here? Are the exchanges making obscene profits?" No, they're not. They're not allowed to do arbitrage. Individuals are doing the arbitrage.

I explained, it's not the bitcoin that's expensive. If I go down the street right now with U.S. dollars and buy bitcoin, the price they will give me is the exact same price I can get in San Francisco. Bitcoin's price is exactly the same. But if I give them rupees, they'll want 22 percent more rupees. It's not bitcoin's price that went up —it's the rupee discount that went up. The rupee price collapsed by 22 percent. Bitcoin can be moved across borders to settle the arbitrage difference but you can't move rupees, you're stuck with them. The fact that you can't move them imposes an immediate 22 percent discount; that money is worth 22 percent less because it is not portable. *Portable* is one of the three characteristics of what makes currency. You just lost one of them. Actually two, because you just demonetized most of it. Rupees are trading at a discount against bitcoin; bitcoin is the stable price. The market is telling you, "This is more real money than that stuff." The market discovers truth and it tells us.

Be ready, because we're going to start hearing this again and again and again as economies collapse, as currencies get into crisis. It's happening even in developed nations, like the European Union. It could happen here in the U.S., who knows? The markets are trying to correct the situation. They're going to create a flow of money going out into bitcoin. **People will start removing their full faith and credit from the system, putting it in safe-haven assets: gold, silver, bitcoin, etc.**

As soon as that happens, you'll start seeing the articles in the news media, the "fake news" telling you about the "fake money." Maybe you can't tell the difference between what is "fake news" and what isn't "fake news,"" but you can *always* tell the difference between what is real money and what is fake money. The easiest way to find out is to go out on the street and ask the market. The market will tell you the truth.

Thank you.

Immutability and Proof-of-Work

im·mu·ta·ble
/ɪˈmjuːtəb(ə)l/

adjective

1. tamper-proof, something that does not change and cannot be changed. *Contemporary Example*: Bitcoin's proof-of-work is a planetary scale,thermodynamically guaranteed, self-evident system of immutability.

Silicon Valley Bitcoin Meetup; Sunnyvale, California; September 2016

Video Link: https://youtu.be/rsLrJp6cLf4

The Scale of Immutability

The topic of today's talk is proof-of-work and the monument of immutability. Specifically, we'll talk about immutability and what that means in this new era of digital currencies, what it means to have a digital system that is unchanging.

Immutability is a tricky concept—first of all, because it doesn't really exist. Everything changes; there is nothing in nature that is forever unchangeable. The universe itself—the vacuum, the particles—everything changes. Nothing is immutable, so immutability is more a philosophical idea, but we do think of it in practical terms. What do we mean when we say "immutable" in practical terms? I like to think of it on a linear scale. On one end, you have something that's very easy to change, and things get progressively harder to change, all the way to the thing that is most difficult to change, the most unchangeable thing; immutability is that side of the scale. So, for practical purposes, we'll define *immutability* in any sense to be the maximum or endpoint of that scale.

On January 3rd, 2009, the scale expanded significantly, the endpoint changed. A new maximum was defined, a new maximum in terms of what it means to be immutable for a digital system. **Nothing is as immutable as bitcoin; bitcoin defines the end of that scale at the moment, so it redefines the term *immutable*.** That has some interesting implications, including that you can't call the things to the left of that "immutable." You can't call them "immutable-ish," you can't call them "kind of immutable." "Immutable-ish" is like pregnant-ish; it only makes sense as the maximum value, not the maximum minus one. *Immutable*, once it's redefined, prevents everything else from being called "immutable" any more.

The Blockchain and Proof-of-Work

Why is bitcoin immutable? What gives bitcoin the characteristics of immutability? What is it that makes it unchangeable? The first answer that comes to mind for most people is "the blockchain." The blockchain makes bitcoin immutable because every block depends on its predecessor, creating an unbreakable chain back to the genesis block, and if you change something it would be noticed. Therefore, it's unchangeable.

That is the wrong answer, because it's not really "the blockchain" that gives bitcoin its immutability. That's a really important nuance to understand. The blockchain makes sure that you can't change something *without anyone noticing*. In security we call that "tamper-evident": if you change it, it is evident. You cannot tamper with it without leaving evidence of your tampering. But there's a higher standard in security. We call it "tamper-proof": something that cannot be tampered with.

  Not just "will be visible if it's tampered with," but "cannot be tampered with." Immutable.

The characteristic that gives bitcoin its tamper-proof capability is not "the blockchain"; it's proof-of-work. Proof-of-work is what makes bitcoin fundamentally immutable. That is a really important concept to understand, because a lot of people are throwing around the word "blockchain" and claiming that their alternative blockchains are immutable even though they don't have a proof-of-work consensus algorithm, or any kind of consensus algorithm that gives them immutability. At best, they are tamper-evident, meaning someone will notice; but they are not unchangeable.

This distinction is going to become historically important.

You may think "historically important" is a pretty heavy term. Why is it going to be "historically important"? Because if bitcoin continues to work the way it's working today, we are introducing a new concept, which is a form of digital history that is forever. If that history lasts 10 years, that's impressive; if it lasts 100 years, that's astonishing; if it lasts 1,000 years, it becomes an enduring monument—an edifice— of immutability. A system of forever, unshakable history that is truly a monument of our civilization. We have to consider the possibility that will happen.

The History of Proof-of-Work

Let's expand the discussion a bit and talk about proof-of-work. Proof-of-work was not invented by Satoshi Nakamoto. You can see evidence of proof-of-work systems throughout human civilization. There is some big pointy proof-of-work in Cairo: the pyramids. There is some big stone proof-of-work in Paris: the Cathedral of Notre Dame. In fact, proof-of-work is something that our civilization does quite often.

Let's think about that for a second. The pyramids served a few purposes: one as a religious artifact; another as a tomb for the king. The even more interesting purpose is a declaration to every civilization and every human who sees it: "Behold, this is the measure of the Egyptian civilization. This is what we can build. This is proof-of-work. You cannot build this in a civilization that doesn't have abundant resources. You cannot build this unless you can support 20,000 people to not do anything *but* this. You cannot build this unless you can guard it with soldiers, unless you commit resources for decades or centuries. This cannot be built cheaply."

The pyramids stand today as a testament of proof-of-work for the Egyptian civilization. Without even understanding what a pyramid is, anyone riding across the desert, on a camel, who crests a hill and sees a stone monument that's a few hundred feet in the air, looks at that and exclaims, "Wow!" "Wow" being an expression of believing the proof-of-work, because they immediately and intuitively understand something great built that and there is no cheap way to do it.

The Cathedral of Notre Dame illustrates the same thing, marshaling thousands of stonemasons over hundreds of years to build a monument to the Church, a monument of religion that made people stand in such awe that many believed it was from divine, and not human, origin. The monument itself says, "Behold the Church and what we can do." That kind of open expenditure of resources to make a point—that is proof-of-work.

We've see this again and again in civilization, but until now we've only seen it in local environments for a specific country, organization, or civilization. **Bitcoin is the first planetary-scale, digital monument of proof-of-work.** To those who come later, we will be able to say, "Behold this monument of immutability built over decades. Marvel at its function as well as its elegance." Because it has function; it serves a practical purpose, and that practical purpose is to become a record of history forever—to become the definitive and authoritative source that cannot be modified, the record of truth that cannot lie. Once a transaction is embedded into the bitcoin blockchain and secured by proof-of-work, it becomes incredibly difficult to change.

The Purpose of Mining Is Security

What does it mean to change the bitcoin blockchain? This is something many people don't really understand. I'm often asked, "Andreas, what if 51 percent of the miners decide to change it? What if there's a consensus attack? What if a well-funded government invests heavily in hashing equipment in order to go back and change the blockchain?" These questions seem similar but they're actually very different, so let's look at a few technical details to help us better understand.

Importantly, there is a huge difference between changing the past and changing the future. The consensus algorithm, as it is, determines the future of the blockchain. If you have a majority of the hashing power on the bitcoin blockchain, you can decide what gets recorded in the future, but you can't so easily change the past. The reason you can't change the past is because every node on the network will still validate every block and demand proof-of-work. That block still has to carry proof-of-work and there is only one way that proof-of-work can be generated: you have to commit energy resources to a particular block.

When you read all of these articles in the media about how "wasteful" bitcoin is, because bitcoin is created by burning energy, they are completely missing the point.

Mining doesn't work to create bitcoin. That is not the purpose of mining; that is a side effect. The way I can prove it's a side effect is that one day, there will be no new bitcoin. But guess what? There will still be mining. Even after the last satoshi (the smallest unit of bitcoin) gets mined, mining continues. It must continue because its purpose is not to create bitcoin but to provide security, to provide validation of all of the transactions and blocks according to the consensus rules. Generating bitcoin is a side effect that currently serves as a mechanism of reward, creating game-theory incentives to make sure that the validation is done right. Once you understand that and you realize what we're paying for is security, it changes the perspective slightly. But it's much deeper than that.

Staking an Extrinsic Asset: Energy

A lot of different consensus algorithms have been proposed; proof-of-stake is one of them. Many of these algorithms use the native asset to stake into the mining algorithm, into the consensus algorithm, meaning I'm going to commit x amount of my currency in validating the next block. If I fail to validate it correctly, I lose that currency; if I validate it correctly, I gain a small fee.

Here's the news: **proof-of-work is also proof-of-stake, but proof-of-stake is *not* also proof-of-work**. Let me explain that a bit more because this is a really important point. Each time a miner creates a candidate block, a specific block, stuffs all of the transactions into that block after carefully validating them, and then hashes against it through the proof-of-work mining algorithm, they are committing to that block, committing resources.

Essentially, they're saying, "I'm staking $100 or $500 worth of electricity behind the security work I have done; if I haven't done it right, I lose my electricity stake." So, proof-of-work *is* proof-of-stake, because what you're staking is the energy investment committed behind a specific block that you've validated correctly. To prove that you have validated it correctly, you are staking an enormous amount of electricity behind it, electricity that costs money.

Notice, though, that this is different from proof-of-stake algorithms in other digital currencies. The difference here is that what you're staking is not a native asset, something intrinsic to the chain whose value and future is determined by the chain. What you're staking here is something extrinsic to the system: you're staking energy—something that has universal value on this planet.

The value of an intrinsic currency tomorrow may be nothing, in which case the value of the stake you made is nothing. But the value of the electricity today, tomorrow, into the foreseeable future, is something. That means that when you're staking electricity, you're staking something that has value throughout our planet. Proof-of-work is a lot deeper than we initially realize.

Rewriting the Past: Consensus Attacks Explained

What if the miners decide to a do a 51-percent attack to rewrite the past? Instead of starting from the current block and changing the rules into the future, what if they start from a previous block and mine forward? If they have 51 percent of the hashing power, they will eventually reach the current block in the minority chain and exceed it. They will win the race. Eventually. The question is, how long do they have to sustain the attack in order to win?

Let's take a simple scenario: let's say we want to go back and change history 3 weeks ago. Three weeks doesn't seem like a long time; in bitcoin, it's an eternity. Every day, 500 megawatts of electricity are used continuously to feed the mining process (a ballpark figure, might be more or less). Five hundred megawatts in 24 hours is 12 gigawatt hours of electricity expended per day. Twelve gigawatt hours of electricity over 30 days is 360 gigawatt hours of electricity. Over 12 months, that's 4.3 terawatt hours of electricity. In a year, 4.3 terawatt hours of electricity is a lot of electricity, but it's only a lot of electricity if you take it all at once. If you take it on a daily 500-megawatt basis running forward, it's enough to keep the bitcoin network secure. But here's the thing: if you try to change the past in bitcoin, it starts adding up pretty fast.

How long will it take to re-mine the blocks of the last 3 weeks with 51 percent of the hashing power? At 100 percent of the hashing power, it takes 3 weeks to mine 3,000 blocks. You might think that with 51 percent of the hashing power it will take 6 weeks to mine 3,000 blocks. However, it will actually take 5 weeks. It will take 4 weeks to mine the first 2,000 blocks with approximately half the hashing power, but once 2016 blocks have been mined, the mining difficulty will change. It will only take one more week to mine the last 1,000 blocks. So, it will end up taking approximately 5 weeks total to re-mine 3 weeks' worth of blocks with about 51 percent of the hashing power.

Here's the problem: the other side didn't stop mining. The miners remaining on the 49 percent side have mined 3,000 additional blocks, they're not rewriting history, they've continued to extend the original chain. After 5 weeks of this battle, the 51 percent side is still 3,000 blocks behind. They've rewritten the past, and now they're stuck in the past, trying to catch up with an advantage of only 2 percent.

Meanwhile, the miners who are on the 51 percent side are earning nothing. Presumably, they already had 51 percent of the hashing power when they were mining the first time around, and now that they're trying to re-mine the last 3 weeks of blocks, they've already banked the rewards but on the other chain which they're now trying to make invalid. Of course they're going to get rewards on the new chain, but only if they give up the rewards that they banked on the other chain.

Effectively, they're going to spend weeks and weeks mining at 500 megawatts for free.

Meanwhile, what happens on the other chain? You're a 49-percent miner and the first 2016 blocks are going to be slow; you'll only be finding blocks approximately every 20 minutes. But your share of the mining capacity just doubled, which means your profitability just doubled. You'll earn twice the reward for the same amount of mining. If that chain still has value, you're making quite a bit of money because you now have a bigger market share. In fact, the more people who abandon the chain, the more profitable it is for the minority. All you have to do is peel off 2 percent; all you have to do is persuade 2 percent of the people mining for nothing to come mine on the chain where you're mining for double the rewards. How hard is that going to be?

Sustaining a 51-percent attack for weeks is brutally hard. Of course, that means you'd probably only do it if you had 75-80 percent of the hashing power. Ethereum started with 90 percent and at some point went as low as 70 percent on the majority chain when they did their fork in 2016; that's a pretty big drop.

Please notice that I've been talking about changing only *3 weeks* of history. But bitcoin is 7 years old. What if you wanted to change a transaction that was last year? A year and a half ago? Well, now the math is *really* against you because it's going to take you more than a year to overtake that chain, during which time you have to sustain that attack and not lose anyone from your group. Otherwise, you never overtake it and make even less money. Effectively, you will have staked your electricity twice and at most you will only be rewarded once.

Unforgeable Artifacts

The bitcoin blockchain is a monument of immutability, built block by block, and these blocks are now towering into the sky—420,000 of them—containing a cumulative amount of work that is absolutely gobsmacking. It cannot be changed or forged, without not only the other person *knowing* it has been changed but without you actually expending the energy all over again; there is no shortcut. That is the difference between *tamper-evident* and *tamper-proof*.

Bitcoin is not simply a system of accounting; it is the first digital artifact that provides forever-history, that provides true digital immutability. There is no other system that provides digital immutability at that level. **It is a planetary-scale, thermodynamically-guaranteed, self-evident system of immutability.** *Planetary-scale*, because in order to do it you need to marshal resources that only exist in a planetary-scale effort. *Thermodynamically-guaranteed*, because you can calculate the exact amount of energy it took to create it and there is no shortcut. Information theory tells us that to flip x number of bits, it takes this y number of joules, and there is no way to do it otherwise. *Self-evident*, because the number that is produced as proof-of-work tells you exactly how much work has been done cumulatively. It really is a monument.

Better Than Written in Stone: Immutability as a Service

There is nothing else on the planet that produces a digital record which is self-evidently immutable at this scale. Nothing. It is the only platform on which you can embed data that will be guaranteed immutable within a few blocks. A thousand blocks after you put data in, there's no going back; that data is not going to change. Maybe if you put it in, and it's only three blocks old, it could change. Six blocks old? Eh... One hundred and forty-four? This is getting tough—and that's a day. A week old? A month? A year? Two years? Done: it's part of permanent history.

Our ancestors said, "This is as good as written in stone." Our grandchildren will say, "It is as good as written on the blockchain." This is the new standard of immutability, and it is globally accessible. Any application can leverage that capability; other currencies, other chains, smart contracts, they can all checkpoint against the bitcoin blockchain. As long as we continue to build the monument, their little inscription—like a piece of graffiti etched into the base stones of the pyramids —will be there, potentially for centuries. They can import immutability for the low price of a transaction fee.

Immutability as a service is an astonishing application. It has enormous implications for software, for the Internet of Things, for information security, for other systems of currency, for systems of record (title, registration, birth records, etc). History can be written on the blockchain and as long as it's there, it cannot be changed and everyone can validate it.

That is not a waste of electricity; that is the first practical application of digital immutability. It is expensive, but it is expensive because it's giving us something valuable on a planetary scale. We only need one proof-of-work immutable ledger; it's probably too expensive to build two. But that just means that the network effect is even more awesome, because we already have one and it's doing quite well. One can support all of the other applications; the other applications could do the much more lightweight proof-of-stake. But if the other applications really want immutability—not tamper-evident, but tamper-proof—they need to get that service from the bitcoin blockchain; they need to anchor their data to the bitcoin blockchain.

We Don't Do 1984 on the Bitcoin Blockchain

If you're a banking consortium, and you are signing transactions in a distributed ledger technology by taking turns, what is the cost of fabricating the past? What is the cost of rewriting history, of saying, "WikiLeaks never received any of your donations because we reversed all of those transactions"? What is the cost of that? Thermodynamically, nothing. In on-chain money? Doesn't matter, because you created the on-chain money and you can create more of it.

As long as there is no proof-of-work behind it, the cost of rewriting a ledger like that is zero. If you can, you will. If you can, you'll be coerced to. If you can, when you get a subpoena, you must. These blockchains are not immutable; they're mutable as hell! They're fickle blockchains—they belong on the opposite side of the scale. They're transient, meaningless, with no weight of history behind them; they are whatever the last signer says they are. This year: "We're at war with Oceania." Next year: "We've always been at war with Eastasia." History is written by the victors. Not on the bitcoin blockchain. We don't do *1984* on the bitcoin blockchain.

Now history is written by the expenditure of real-world energy, and there is no cheap way to forge that history.

Thank you.

Note from Andreas to the reader: In this talk I foolishly attempted to improvise math in my head while delivering the talk. I am not very good at math. Turns out I am even worse at improv-math. None of my bad math changes the point I was making, but it's been edited for accuracy and to protect my ego. Ssssh! Don't tell anyone I suck at improv-math.

Hard Promises, Soft Promises

YOUR MONEY* IS SAFE*, WE PROMISE*

* "Your money": is no longer your money,
it is an unsecured 0% interest loan to us
*S.A.F.E. (Subject to Appropriation Fofeiture
or Embrezzlement) without notice.
S.A.F.E. (TM) is a registered trademark of
BigBank Corp. and should not be interpreted
to imply the security or availability of funds.
* "promise": all promises valid unless subordinated
to terms and conditions, judicial supboena, whim,
act of god, act of war, act of government, act of us,
except where void by statute, treaty, obligation, pirates, godzilla,
natural disaster or a mild summer breeze.

San Francisco Bitcion Meetup; San Francisco, California; September 2016

Video Link: https://youtu.be/UJSdMFPjW8c

The Patented Editable Blockchain

Is everybody here really excited about distributed ledger technology and what it can do for banking?

Earlier today, Accenture announced a patent they filed for the first editable blockchain that can be modified, resolving the fundamental problem we had in bitcoin of immutability. With their contribution, and the contributions of other companies like that, one by one we can solve the fundamental problems in bitcoin, such as decentralization, open access, lack of a central authority or counterparty risk, immutability, and, at some point, I'm assuming, the concept of sound money.

They invented something new, the editable blockchain. I'm really glad some consultant got paid probably a couple million dollars to invent that. You know, for that kind of price they had to give it a really good name, because "spreadsheet" was already taken!

Predictability Outside of Human Society

As new people join bitcoin and open-blockchain communities, they often look at bitcoin, at these open, borderless, decentralized, censorship-resistant systems, and the systems are so alien they can't quite grasp why they are the way they are. And so their first instinct is to "fix" them.

One of the most common themes we've been hearing lately is that the fundamental problem with open blockchains is that they are immutable, that the transactions are irreversible. That will be the topic of today's talk: hard promises.

Why is this a problem? It's because we're not accustomed to hard promises. Very few things in life are guaranteed; outcomes are not predictable. There's a Chinese saying: "The sun, the moon, and the truth will not be hidden for long." If you think of the things we can expect in a predictable pattern, we have to look outside of human society. We have to look at things that are not affected by human emotion, relationships or agreements. We have to look at math, at physics, at the stars. Those things are predictable, unalterable.

Bitcoin uses mathematics to introduce the concept of unalterable, predictable outcomes into a payment system. This is totally alien because we've never done it in financial systems before, and the initial reaction to that is often, "Well, that's broken."

New Systems of Hard Promises and Programmable Money

But this new system isn't broken; it's just that there is a fundamental misunderstanding about what a bitcoin transaction is, and what it means for a transaction to be irreversible. If you think a bitcoin transaction is a payment, then the concept of an irreversible payment seems a bit weird, scary even. What if you make a mistake? Who do you appeal to? How do you get a refund? What is the process?

But a bitcoin transaction isn't a payment; a bitcoin transaction is a program, and it's not the *payment* that is irreversible—it's the *program* that is irreversible.

Bitcoin gives you the ability to take a program and have that program execute exactly as written, guaranteed with all of its parameters, and that is unalterable. Once it's been specified by the sender, that program will execute exactly as specified, predictably, everywhere the same. It cannot be appealed, reversed, or censored.

If you write a program to say, "I'm paying John, whom I've never met in my life, to ship me something via UPS," and then John (who isn't actually named John) doesn't ship, that program will still execute. Now you've got something rather problematic, an irreversible payment. But you don't have to write the program exactly like that. In fact, within the programs inside bitcoin, we can implement all kinds of layers. **What bitcoin gives us is a hard promise: the program will execute exactly as specified.**

The beauty in distributed systems is, if you start with a foundation that offers you a hard promise, a system of constraints on what will happen, you can relax those. You can loosen that promise. You can write a script that says, "I will pay John, based on a multisignature transaction with a third-party escrow agent and an automated refund in 30 days, unless a signature from UPS shows that the package was delivered and no dispute has occurred in the meantime." Not so scary anymore.

The payment script can include all of the consumer protection you want, with a few fundamental differences. The sender chooses the counterparty; it's not selected for them. The recourse is specified in advance, and it is guaranteed as a hard promise that cannot be violated by anyone—not John, not some other third party, some intermediary, and not by some authority that wasn't involved in the original transaction.

You take a hard promise and, because it's programmable money, you soften it to introduce exactly the measure of consumer protection that the parties want. They have full control over the terms.

The Current System of Soft Promises

While distributed systems have hard constraints that can be softened, you can't say the opposite. A system that only delivers soft promises can never deliver a hard promise. If you have a system of payments that is subject to review, revision, censorship, authorities, courts, others—that system can never guarantee anything. Every promise it delivers can be broken; every promise can be reversed.

How many people here have money in the bank? None of you has money in the bank. You have all extended a mostly unsecured loan for a pathetic level of interest, to a bank that is holding that money as their own and using it to earn very high interest from other people. Maybe, if you walk up to an ATM or bank teller, you can get some of that back. Unless you're Greek, Argentinian, Cyprian, Venezuelan, Ukrainian, Brazilian... The list goes on and on through the decades, because those promises are soft.

You can appeal to a system of courts where the "ironclad rule of law" will deliver swift, efficient justice to all. Maybe in *this* country. For how many countries is that not even a consideration? What is the difference between those countries and this country? They know the rule of law is a myth; they know that money, influence, connections, political power and, at the end of it, violence can override the rule of law. Here, the difference is **we still believe the illusion that the rule of law delivers justice for all**. But those who benefit from it the most are quite clear that even here, money, influence, political power, connections, can swiftly override the rule of law.

Today, the head of Wells Fargo was testifying in front of Congress. Over a period of a decade, the entire consumer-credit department fabricated credit lines without the consent of the customers. Fabricating PINs and lines of credit, damaging credit ratings, creating spurious charges, all to drive the bottom line. That fraud earned the CEO $200 million in capital appreciation.

You'll be pleased to know that that CEO, as we speak, is facing jail time... No, of course he isn't! Come on, where have you been? No, he fired 5300 low-level, $12-an-hour employees. The head of the department walked away with $125 million in severance and Wells Fargo was fined $185 million, which isn't even the profit that one person, the CEO, made over this 10-year period. Nothing will happen, and this is in the most over-regulated, protected industry, with oversight and Congressional hearings, in the country with the most stellar record of the rule of law.

Soft promises, empty promises.

The False Narrative of Chaos Without Authority

When you see people who are complaining about the fact that bitcoin can deliver hard promises, you have to start thinking, *What are they afraid of?* **What, exactly, is so terrifying about a system that records things on a blockchain in a way that no one can modify, that creates unalterable and predictable outcomes?**

When they speak about it, they conjure up these images of defrauded consumers and chaos. "*Après moi, le déluge*" ("After me, the flood"), King Louis XV warned his subjects if they had a revolution. He was authority and in the absence of authority, anarchy would prevail. During the Revolutionary War here, King George III warned his subjects, "I am order. On the other side, privateers, murderers, and scoundrels like George Washington are going to lead you into chaos"—implying that without authority, the alternative is chaos.

This narrative has infected minds for centuries. This narrative assumes that the human condition lies on a single line where, down and to the left, there is zero order, zero authority; as you go up the line, authority leads to order. If you believe in this, then the idea of a system that has no authority automatically equates with sliding down the line into chaos, disorder.

I have news for you: it's not a line, it's a Cartesian plane. **The opposite of authority is autonomy.** What the blockchain demonstrates is a system that substitutes authority with autonomy. What it gives us is *not* chaos; what it gives us is the *highest* of order, which we have never seen before. It gives us predictable outcomes that are not subject to the whim of authority.

If you're on that line, you can't see that there are other options, and we see societies destroyed by this very fake trade-off, because when order starts to diminish in a society, the people call for more authority. We know where that ends. More authority and more authority; that authority corrupts, and then eventually it kills. In Venezuela, we're seeing the end result today: maximum authority, complete collapse of social order. The line flattens, where authority is maximum and order is zero.

And what do the leaders ask for? More authority.

A Future with Unalterable Systems

This technology allows us to re-envision the social order, creating systems that —instead of authority—use autonomy to deliver order. But it's better than that, because this form of order is unprecedented. Imagine that every individual has the ability, when they create a transaction, to specify exactly the conditions under which that transaction will be executed and then be absolutely guaranteed that those conditions will be met. What is the value of that to individuals? What kind of world does that create? It certainly creates a world in which the people who are clinging to authority are both terrified and, more importantly, irrelevant.

But we've seen this before. What other systems create outcomes that cannot be changed? One of my favorite examples comes from the internet. We are about 10 or 15 years into realizing that the internet has a quirk we hadn't considered; it, too, creates a set of unalterable outcomes. Once something is published on the internet, it cannot be unpublished. We're now the first generation living with the reality that what happens on the internet stays forever on the internet. It cannot be removed, it cannot be censored; the more you try, the more it propagates.

This has not been received lightly by those in authority. In many countries today, there is a desperate fight to ensure that things can be unpublished; that is a losing fight because they can't.

The internet has given us a glimpse of what it means to have an unalterable system. Who has it affected most? Has it affected us, who are becoming aware of this and being much more careful, flexible about what we publish? Or has it affected those in authority who do not want their secrets, their lies, their crimes, revealed and published on a system that cannot be silenced? The internet gives us a glimpse of what it means to create unalterable outcomes. We have no idea how valuable this property is; I think it's extremely valuable.

So why, in this environment, would you create a mutable ledger? Because it brings back the comfort of authority. But what it also does is it feeds the legitimacy, the power, and the control of whatever hierarchy or organization you've put in place to decide what gets altered and what doesn't.

The bitcoin blockchain gives us a network-centric system where there is no authority and the outcomes are predictable. To replace that, you have to put in place a very traditional industrialized society model of hierarchies and appeals and positions of power, where they get to decide what gets written and more importantly what gets erased. History is written by the victors. This is going to be sold to people as a way to protect your own safety. You're not good enough, smart enough, sophisticated enough to decide what program you want to embed in your transactions, to create unalterable outcomes. You need protection.

Hard Promises Feed Autonomy

We already have a system that gives us reversible transactions; it gives us a system of appeals, of recourse. Whose transactions get reversed? How many times does a transaction, which takes money out of your pocket and puts it in the pocket of someone who works in a banking institution or position of authority, get reversed? How many times does a transaction, where you're trying to contribute to a political cause or a political party—or donate to WikiLeaks—get reversed?

How many times is the mechanism of recourse used as a mechanism of control?

That is the inevitable outcome when you build a hierarchy and they get to decide what gets written and what gets erased. They write the things that fill their pockets and erase the things that offend them.

The current system of recourse doesn't protect consumers; it's not even a factor for most consumers. When Wells Fargo debits your account $35 to open a credit card that you never asked for, it takes 10 years and a Congressional inquiry and *maybe* you'll get your $35 back. *Maybe* they'll fix your credit score. But no one will go to jail.

Soft promises feed hierarchy. Hard promises feed autonomy. **What we've built with bitcoin is a system of hard promises that can be softened to give you all the flexibility you'd need to do your own consumer protection, on your own terms that you specify.** That is terrifying to those who are in a position of authority—and it's absolutely exhilarating to everybody else.

Thank you.

The Currency Wars

Coinscrum Minicon at Imperial College; London, England; December 2016

Video Link: https://youtu.be/Bu5Mtvy97-4

Remittances, Not the First Application of Bitcoin

Today I'm going to talk about currency wars and bitcoin's neutrality in those currency wars.

You've probably heard me say that I believe some of the first applications we would see in bitcoin would relate to foreign remittances and cross-border applications such as import/export and trade. Because these are areas where there is friction in the traditional financial system, systems like bitcoin, which are much more flexible, could provide opportunities—especially opportunities for underprivileged people around the world. Specifically, immigrants using foreign remittances, where they're paying extravagant fees to transmit through traditional channels like Western Union.

Well, it turns out I was wrong. Not the first time, not the last; it's going to happen again. But let's see why I was wrong because this is where things get interesting.

The Currency Wars Have Begun

Bitcoin doesn't exist in a vacuum. Bitcoin is a currency and a system of payment that exists in a highly competitive world of international finance that accounts for trillions of dollars in payments every single year, in 194 countries. While we're off in our little corner, designing great applications for bitcoin, something else has happened that I think will change the trajectory of adoption of bitcoin. We're going to see some very exciting times ahead.

What has happened over the last two years is we're now seeing a full-fledged global currency war. This war started, in a small way, just after the financial crisis in 2008 and it's been gaining speed. This currency war is going to change the trajectory of bitcoin; something that happened *outside* bitcoin is going to change how bitcoin deploys.

These currency wars have billions of people as hostages, being tossed around like pawns in a geopolitical game. Let me throw out some names of countries and you see if you can see something in common: Greece, Cyprus, Spain, Venezuela, Argentina, Brazil, India, Turkey, Pakistan, the Ukraine. What do these countries have in common? Wonderful people and great food, yes, but they each are also currently embroiled in either a domestic or an international currency war. **The people in these countries are hostages in these currency wars.**

India's War on Cash

If you've been paying attention to the news recently, you may know that approximately 5 weeks ago the Indian government announced that the two largest denominations of bills, the 500-rupee and the 1,000-rupee, would no longer be legal tender and would cease to be legal tender *in 4 hours*. Thus removing 86 percent of cash in circulation by value, in a country where *more than 95 percent of all transactions happen in cash* and where more than 40 percent of the population has no bank account.

The immediate effect is expected to be a loss of about 2-4 percent of the GDP of the country. But the ripple effect has been devastating. We've seen entire industries in India crawl to a halt, because employers aren't able to pay employees, people are unable to buy food or health care, they're unable to transact. It has been an absolute disaster in the short term and will likely be a continuing disaster in the long term.

The Global War on Cash

Make no mistake: this is an experiment with 15 percent of humanity as experimental subjects. If this experiment is successful—not in terms of how these people fare but whether the aims of government are achieved—this experiment will be repeated. It will be repeated in many countries just like the experiment of bail-ins in Cyprus was exported to other countries. These experiments are accelerating.

Now there is global war on cash. We have reached that point in history where it is within the grasp, within the vision, of world governments, once and for all, to eradicate cash. Cash—being the ultimate peer-to-peer, transparent, private form of money that allows individuals to transact locally within a community—is now being eradicated in favor of digital transactions on platforms that allow for surveillance, control, confiscation, and negative interest rates. All of these things will follow very closely once cash is no longer part of the picture. That's their dream.

I hope you'll be joining me in ruining that dream.

The International Currency War

In addition to the war on cash, there is another currency war happening now-- an international currency war. In this war, nation is pitted against nation using its flag money, its national currency, as a trade-war instrument in order to tip the trade balance and erode the national debt in countries that are suffering from enormous debt loads they have no hope of ever paying back.

If you are a government and you have debt measured in the billions or trillions of dollars, how do you best pay back that debt? By increasing standards of living and productivity until you can grow yourself out of it? Or by confiscating the savings of retirees and the middle class, destroying a generation of workers, and having them pay the debt through a shadow tax, inflation? We know which side countries are choosing, because we're seeing this play out again and again.

Of course, that's not how they sell it. They don't say, "Our plan to exit the debt is to destroy pensioners and the middle class and create a system of shadow taxation and confiscation to bail out the banks and bail out the government debt." What they say instead is, "This will eradicate black money, this will permanently end corruption, and we will win the war on crime!" And most people say, "Hey, that sounds like a great idea! Let's go for it."

The Politics of Wealth Destruction

This false promise is almost always wrapped in popular nationalism. The great scourge of the emerging 21st century is the resurgence of populist nationalism. Fascism is rising. Just as the politicians wrap themselves in the flag, they also create these associations with their national flag money, to wrap their money in the veil of nationalism, to wrap the policies of wealth destruction and confiscation in the veil of nationalism.

If you disagree with the idea that pensioners should pay for the national debt and to bail out the banks, if you disagree with the idea that a whole generation of young people should find themselves permanently unemployed or underemployed or working in "McJobs," then you are a traitor to the nationalist ideal of solving crime and black money and corruption. They'll say, "You probably have some corrupt money hidden, don't you? That must be what motivates you."

That is *exactly* the tone of discussion that is happening right now in places like Turkey, where the government announced that it was everybody's duty as a Turkish citizen to sell their dollars and buy lira and gold in order to prop up the nationalist pride. Where the same exact rationale was used in India to get everyone to "suffer just a little bit." Remember the people suffering the most have no voice, they are invisible—especially in India. The middle class that suffers, just a little bit, can wrap itself in the flag, in these nationalist ideals.

Bitcoin, the Safe Haven

In these currency wars, there is one force that stands neutral as a safe haven, as an exit strategy. **Bitcoin is now standing on the precipice of becoming the safe-haven asset for billions of people around the world** who, for the first time, will have the opportunity to say, "You know what? I see where you're going. You go ahead. I'm opting out."

That's going to dramatically change the trajectory of bitcoin; it's going to change the technology and the economics of bitcoin. It's going to change the attitude of those in power towards bitcoin. Foreign remittances is something a government can get behind. Governments can easily say, "Yes! Let's make it easier for our poor immigrants abroad to send money to this country while kind of competing with the banks to the degree we allow them through regulation." But this new proposition—that some people are going to get to opt out from these crazy nationalist experiments and currency wars—is not going to be taken lightly.

Bitcoin is going to represent, in many of these countries, a direct affront to sovereignty. When sovereigns see a direct challenge to their rule, to their decisions—as arbitrary, capricious, and unilateral as their decisions may be, as unconcerned with the consent of the governed they may be—they will apply their full force in order to fight that threat. They will fail, but it's not going to be easy.

Escaping the Currency Wars

When these things start happening, the equilibrium between currencies changes; we've already started seeing this. If you want to buy bitcoin in India today, be prepared to pay more than $1,000 USD. The premium on bitcoin has reached 22 percent higher than the price in any other market. It can't easily be arbitraged away because there isn't a big enough flow of bitcoin into the country to counterbalance the mad scramble to the exits that is happening.

The Chinese yuan has been devalued six times so far in 2016. And every time the Chinese yuan was devalued, bitcoin's value went up by about a billion dollars, as millions of Chinese opted out and took the exit.

Every time this happens, a premium is paid. But here's the good news: guess who earns that premium? Those who are willing to build an exit sign and a door, a little muddy road that leads out of the crazy nationalist experiments, get to earn a 20 percent premium. The exchanges, the LocalBitcoins traders, the off-chain, offline underground traders, those willing to take the risk and face the wrath of the sovereign, earn a premium. That premium goes directly to funding infrastructure development, liquidity, stealthiness, decentralization, evasion, and all of the other things that might be necessary to allow average people to get the hell out of the currency war.

These experiments are going to position governments directly in opposition to bitcoin, not because of something bitcoin did, but because of something the governments have done themselves.

Playing God

When I was growing up, I really enjoyed computer games. One of my favorite computer games was SimCity. One of the things about SimCity that was really cool was that you had full and unilateral control of the economy; one of the dials you could tweak was the income tax. It was always tempting to tweak tax rates, especially if your budget wasn't quite balancing or things weren't going quite as well as you wanted in the game. If you couldn't build as fast as you wanted, you could just raise the income tax from 5 percent to 6 percent, from 6 percent to 7 percent.

There were consequences, of course. One of the ways you learned about those consequences was when you went too far. If you raised tax from 5 percent to 15 percent, at first you'd fill your coffers as the income tax started flying in. Then you'd watch your population plummet as everybody left your city. Those kinds of games have a name: they're called "god games," and the reason they're so satisfying to play is because they allow you to play god over a helpless population.

There were other interesting features, too: you could build an entire city and then launch a tornado, an earthquake, a massive fire, a tsunami, or even a Godzilla attack, on your city. And guess what? None of those attacks was as successful at draining your city than raising the income tax.

The Cost of War

These currency wars are wars on populations. They are a form of civil war from the government against its own people. They destroy generations. It's estimated that already in the first few days in India, people died because they couldn't access money for health treatments, because they had to wait in line—feeble, disabled, elderly—for 6 hours in order to withdraw the equivalent of $30, if they owned that much. More people will probably die just in the next few weeks as this experiment unfolds. And this repeats. Tens of thousands of people have died in Venezuela because of currency wars, because of the destruction of the monetary system.

This is what happens when governments decide that the way to fight a trade war is to use the very fuel of the economy, the thing that people depend on in order to build a future for themselves, as a weapon against another government. That weapon backfires and kills their own people.

The Greatest Form of Terrorism

They will tell you that we are traitors to our nation by encouraging people to use bitcoin. They will tell you that we are criminals, thugs, drug dealers, and terrorists.

Don't believe me? Look up what the Indian government has said just in the last two weeks about people who trade gold on the black market: "terrorists," "criminals," "thugs."

I'm just a coder, I'm just a talker; I'm not a terrorist, I'm not a thug. But if I have the opportunity to build an exit from this system, then I will take that opportunity—because I know who the real terrorists are. **There is no greater form of terrorism than creating war against your own people, by deliberately disrupting the very lifeblood of an economy, when there is no crisis; creating a natural disaster of enormous proportions simply to fight a currency war against another country.**

Who benefits in the end? The banks. They get bailed in. Their balance sheets in India are soaring; their stock prices are soaring. The government: enormous increases in revenue. Does that stop corruption? No. It's fueled an absolute orgy of corruption, just like it fueled an orgy of corruption in Cyprus, Greece, Venezuela, Argentina, and the Ukraine.

When the Indian government announced that the currency would not be legal tender in 4 hours, they also announced that the banks would be closed for two days in order to prevent people from initiating a run on the banks. When the banks opened two days later, miraculously, a significant portion of the cash reserves they had were only in the bad notes. Somehow, some people had access to these vaults and swapped their money—while the banks were closed. Somehow.

Gresham's Law

One fascinating principle in economics is Gresham's Law, which states that bad money chases out good money in an economy. In college, I studied economics just as a hobby, and I didn't really understand Gresham's Law; fortunately, I had never seen Gresham's Law in action. Today, we are watching Gresham's Law play out exactly as predicted.

When an Indian person goes to an ATM, when a Venezuelan manages to get money, when a Zimbabwean gets hold of U.S. dollars, what do they do with that money? Do they spend it? Hell no they don't. They bury it, they put it under the mattress, they hide it, they save it, because this is the good money and it immediately exits the economy.

They take every shitty note they have—every Zimbabwean $100-trillion bond note, every Venezuelan bolivar that's worth nothing, carried in wheelbarrows and weighed by the pound because nobody has time to count it, every 500-rupee note that is now worthless—and they go to their employees and their dependents, their homeworkers and cleaners, the people who aren't privileged in the economy, and they say, "This is the only money I'm going to pay you with. Here's 6 months of wages in advance. Take it or you're fired. Your choice." They offload the bad money onto the people who then have to go and spend 6 hours in line to exchange it, to be asked questions about where they got this money by the evil tax official, the caricature of the government employee.

Guess what they use to pay the government employees for their bribes? The same bad money. So, the bad money is the only money that's circulating and the good money has completely disappeared from the economy. We're watching Gresham's Law in action.

Building the Exit Road

When the people get bitcoin, they're going to *HODL*, which is a colloquial bitcoin community term which means holding bitcoin long term. When they get bitcoin, they're going to bury it so deep to make sure that they have the good money saved for their children, for their future. They're going to trade the bad money for bitcoin, and nowadays all money is bad money.

Cash is being eradicated around the world as a scourge. But they can't win that game, because cash is now something that the people can create—electronic cash, self-sovereign cash, verifiable cash, digital cash, peer-to-peer cash. Bitcoin.

Remember, this is going to change the trajectory of bitcoin deployment over the next two years. It's going to be in direct opposition to this currency war and it's going to be directly funded by the currency war. The currency wars are going to fund investment in infrastructure and improvements in bitcoin, creating that small exit sign and the little rutted road behind it.

Over the next few years as these currency wars escalate and escalate and escalate —as they will, as they must, as they fail and try again—we're going to widen that rutted road until eventually we are offering from every economy an eight-lane Autobahn highway exit out of their currency war, for everyone to be able to take.

It won't be available for everyone at first. It will be only the richest, the most educated, the privileged, the ones who have access to these applications. But somewhere in there, they're going to take some other people with them. Gradually, they're going to fund the infrastructure that is going to allow more and more people to exit from these economies.

We Didn't Start the Fire

Remember that as this happens, we're going to be called criminals for offering an exit. Then we're going to be called criminals for pointing at the exit. Then we're going to be called criminals for simply pointing out the fact that the economy is on fire and there is an exit.

At each stage of escalation in the currency wars, every act you take in opposition to the observable fact that the entire economy is on fire, every chance you give people to head for the exit, you will be labeled a criminal. Before long, they will rewrite history to say that the reason the banks are failing and the economy is on fire is because you provided an exit and because bitcoin exists. **They will say that bitcoin started the fire.**

At that point, remember the slogan and repeat it: "We are not criminals. We're offering an exit for everybody. We didn't start the fire"

Thank you.

Bubble Boy and the Sewer Rat

DevCore Workshop at Draper University; San Mateo, California; October 2015

Video Link: https://youtu.be/810aKcfM__Q

Purell Parenting, Mud Cakes, and Bubble Boys

Today I want to talk about security. If you listen to the trolls on Reddit, I don't know anything about security, so I decided instead that I'll talk about parenting —because I don't have any kids. If I'm going to talk about things I don't know, I might as well start there, right?

Parenting has changed a lot in the last couple of decades. When I grew up, things were very different. My sister just had a baby. I'm watching her as a parent and meeting her parent friends. As an uncle, I feel like a proxy parent; it's really strange.

My sister and I were discussing how when we were growing up, hand sanitizers like Purell didn't exist. And how, by today's standards, it's a miracle we actually survived. Apparently, bacteria is everywhere, and much of today's parenting involves protecting kids from this bacteria with gallon jugs of Purell. If you watch these parents, as soon as their kid touches a bit of dirt, they immediately give him a Purell shower, right there, just to make sure he's clean.

That's not the experience I had; I grew up in the 1970's. We used to play in the garden and roll around in the mud. We'd make mud cakes. Would our parents freak out? No. We'd eat the mud cakes. Would our parents freak out? No, possibly because they weren't around. They'd say, "Get out of the house and come back when the sun goes down." Things have changed.

Recent scientific studies are uncovering a troubling phenomenon: the rates of asthma and allergies are through the roof. It turns out that if you raise a child in a sterile environment, they don't develop a robust immune system. We now know that exposure to bacteria, for example from eating mud cakes in the garden, is how children build robust immune systems.

You can take this to one extreme or the other. For example, many children in the developing world don't have the severe allergic reactions to common medications that children in the developed world do. Why? Because they have *even more* robust immune systems by being exposed to pathogens all the time from the moment they're born, even before they're born. At the other extreme, you have the concept of raising a child in a bubble. Do you remember that story of Bubble Boy? It's a tragic true story about a child without an immune system. There are these medical tragedies, where children are born with compromised immunity or they lose their immunity through some kind of problem; then they have to live in a bubble to stay alive.

You must be wondering, *What the hell is this guy talking about? I thought this was going to be a talk about security and bitcoin, but here we are talking about Bubble Boy and eating mud cakes.* There's a point to this, hang on.

Isolated and Permissioned Blockchains

The reason I'm talking about this is because it has some really important implications in security. You see, if you create a system that is isolated from external influences, it's not that it doesn't have bugs—it's that you don't know about the bugs the system has. If you create a system that is exposed to external attacks all of the time, it's not that it has a lot of bugs—it's just that you know about the bugs it has because you keep finding them. In the process, you fix them; in the process, the system gets stronger.

This leads to a discussion I want to have about an interesting phenomenon currently appearing in the industry: this concept of isolated blockchains and "permissioned ledgers." In my mind, an isolated blockchain is Bubble Boy. It's building a system completely isolated from the world, with the hopes that isolation is going to make it safer. Banks are like a paranoid helicopter parent who wants to shower their kid in Purell because he touched a booger.

Guess what's going to happen to these sanitized ledgers? They're going to get asthma and severe allergies. Eventually, in the worst case, the bubble bursts. At some point, they'll get exposed to the outside world but they have been isolated for so long, that they've developed no immunity whatsoever. When they suddenly get exposed to some horrific deadly thing, like a pollen particle, they die a horrible death. They have such low immunity that they react horribly to something that a properly stimulated, properly raised organism can resist with ease.

The Failure of Security-by-Isolation

This isn't the first time we've had this discussion. In fact, we learned this with the internet; we learned that security-by-isolation, security-by-obscurity, security-by-control-and-perimeters, security-by-trying-to-tamp-down-on-security-research, fails. It fails miserably.

In the early 90s, I was working as an IT consultant to banks, telling them why they should get email servers and connect to "this email thing." They said many of the same things that I hear in bitcoin today, such as: "Well, we don't know anyone who uses email. None of the other banks use email, so who am I going to send email to in the first place? Secondly, the internet is uncontrolled and that's dangerous. Thirdly, our bankers might say something we don't want them to in email; how do we add a long disclosure form at the bottom? What happens if any of our people can communicate with anyone at any moment in time? That's a recipe for chaos, anarchy!" Of course they didn't consider a bit of chaos and anarchy as good things; many of us in this space probably do.

What did the banks and large corporations do with their first attempt to join the internet? Did they connect TCP/IP (Transmission Control Protocol/Internet Protocol) systems directly to the internet and build robust applications that could communicate over TCP/IP? No. They built moats and walls. They implemented perimeter security. They built firewalls and demilitarized zones. They used all of these military analogies to wall themselves in.

Then, what did they deploy behind these walls? Did they deploy the common open-source protocols, capabilities, and applications of the internet? No. They deployed highly denatured, weak equivalents like Outlook and FrontPage. They built intranet websites with stale and obsolete content that was only accessible during working hours through a VPN (Virtual Private Network) with no influence from the outside. They said, "Look! We're doing internet. We're so cutting-edge, we're so hip." That's how they "did internet"; they built highly isolated environments and often labeled them "internet". For a very long time, the prevailing idea was that, by building these isolated environments, they were more secure—because they could control things through the firewall, they could control access to data, creation of data, access to systems.

Now we know that was an illusion. Not only can companies *not* control these things, but in the process of building these isolated systems, they built "Bubble Boy IT." They built IT systems that had no resilience, no immunity. Outlook had bugs and FrontPage had bugs, but they weren't tested on the wild internet very often; much of the time, they lived behind walls. Eventually, someone gets inside the bubble or the thing that's inside the bubble gets outside the bubble.

The problem with bubbles is that you can't trade through them. If you're in business, your business *is* to trade, to engage in commerce. But commerce can't happen in a bubble; the very concept of a bubble is antithetical to commerce. Sure, you can build a firewall but when your salesperson or executives are on the road, they're going to plug into the hotel internet and contract a bunch viruses. When they come back to the office, they'll connect behind the firewall, and those viruses will spread voraciously infecting everyone within the bubble. Bubbles don't work.

Today a whole generation of companies have come to the realization that, in order to be nimble and effective, they can't be HP / EMC / Cisco / Oracle / Microsoft havens of secluded little kingdoms that don't talk to anyone else. First of all, because it's expensive and doesn't work. Secondly, because it's incredibly vulnerable; it doesn't have immunity.

Now we see this generation of nimble, young startups that are true internet companies. Their products, their internal systems, their collaborations—all of it—is out there, naked, on the internet. It happens on GitHub for all the world to see. They use Gmail and collaborate with external email systems all over the world. Their internal systems are external. There's no such thing as internal in the world of the internet. They're building robust applications because, on day one, those applications live in the wild and they're more secure. They learn to live out there on the big, scary internet. Those companies are thriving and they have systems that are much more secure and much more robust.

Bitcoin, the Sewer Rat

You're probably thinking, *Well, if permissioned ledgers and closed intranets are Bubble Boy, then the wild internet and bitcoin are like a kid eating mud cakes. A system that has immunity, something that is exposed to pathogens.* Well, almost. That might have been the analogy I wanted to go for, but you know me—I'll go a bit further.

Bitcoin isn't the kid that eats mud cakes. Bitcoin is a swarm of sewer rats— gnarly things missing eyes, claws, and tails, like those pigeons you see in Trafalgar Square hopping around with this mutant arm stump. And what do they eat? They eat raw sewage, they eat your trash, they eat the most virulent things on the planet. There is nothing in this world that has more strength in its immune system than a New York rat or pigeon. Or even, god forbid, a squirrel. Those things are horrible.

A sewer rat is not going to have allergies. It's not going to sneeze because of a bit of pollen. This thing is already carrying three variations of the plague, and it shrugs it off. That's exactly what bitcoin is. Issues like transaction malleability? The rat evolves.

Attacks, like DDoS (Distributed Denial of Service) on open port 8333? The rat says "Come and get me!" Is anybody trying? Hell yes, everyone is trying, for six years. The best and the brightest, the meanest and the most malicious, are throwing everything they can at this deformed swarm of sewer rats—these thousands of bitcoin nodes who are listening and are exposed to the vagaries of the wild internet. And they survive.

Bubble-Boy Blockchains

What do you think the banks are going to do? They're going to build Bubble-Boy Blockchains. They're going to build permissioned ledgers. Do you think permissioned ledgers suffer from transaction malleability? Hell yes, they do! Do you think altcoins suffer from transaction malleability? Hell yes, they do! They just don't get those things fixed, and neither will the permissioned ledgers. That's just one of the thousands and thousands of bugs, weaknesses, weird exceptions, and edge cases that we're going to find while living out there in the wild. We're building an incredibly robust system which is already taking shape today.

Beyond the idea that you could have a decentralized consensus system, the idea that that decentralized consensus system could actually survive for six years is kind of ludicrous. The only reason the banks have now gotten to the point of thinking about permissioned ledgers is because they have finally reached the stage of bargaining—the third stage in the five stages of grief for the industry they're about to lose.

Banks' 5 Stages of Grief

They start with denial. The basis of denial is: "This thing isn't going to work, it's going to die any day soon." And it doesn't. Then they say, "It's just silly money and it doesn't have any value." Until it does. "Nobody else is going to play with it." Except that they are. "Serious investors won't put any money in this." Except that they did. And it still refuses to die. They move from denial to bargaining. Somewhere in between, there might be some anger. There will be some depression. Eventually, they'll reach acceptance, but it's going to take a long time.

If you look at the internet, we're now on maybe 25 years in terms of really beginning to broaden its use; 25 years in, and there are plenty of companies out there that think as long as they put their HP / EMC / Cisco / Oracle / Microsoft shit behind a perimeter fence firewall, all is going to be well. They are still building Bubble Boys and intranets on the internet. They haven't learned that lesson after 25 years and it's going to take longer in finance.

Decentralization, open protocols, open source, collaborative development, living in the wild—these aren't just *features* of bitcoin; they are the whole point. If you take a permissioned ledger and say, "That's all nice, we like the database part of it. Can we have it without the open, decentralized, peer-to-peer, open-source, non-controlled, distributed nature of it?" Well, you just threw out the baby with the bath water. You're never going to build a bubble strong enough to secure financial information.

Pop Goes the Bubble

Ironically, this is all happening at the same time that, as banks are finally getting onto the internet, they're leaking. They're leaking from every orifice. Anonymous,

WikiLeaks, insiders—all of that stuff. Banks don't have Confidential Transactions; they don't have encryption, they don't have privacy, they don't have zero-knowledge. They have completely open ledgers, and what do they overlay on top of them? Know Your Customer (KYC) and Anti-Money Laundering (AML). They attach identities to everything they're doing so that when that database gets leaked, it will have a completely rich history not only of every transaction but of every participant in the system. That's what they're building: they're building panopticons of financial information and it's leaking.

The truth of panopticons is, when you build a panopticon, someone stares back. When it's the internet that's staring back, that's 4 billion pairs of eyes. I'm not so worried about my financial information from my bank leaking, because maybe a couple hundred people are going to stare back. But when Angela Merkel's phone numbers and phone calls leak, everybody is staring. Three days ago, the internal presentations and PowerPoints of the U.S. Department of Defense, about their drone assassination program, leaked. You built a panopticon? Four billion pairs of eyes are staring back.

The real question we should be asking about permissioned ledgers is: do you really want to put KYC/AML on Bubble Boy? If you add all of that information, and the database leaks 4, 5, 6, 10 years into the future, you're going to give Anonymous and WikiLeaks historians a complete record of every transaction you ever did. The secret slush budget of Lockheed Martin. The black budget of your government. The bribes that you paid to depose a democratically elected government or to install an oil well in a pristine rainforest. All of that shit is going to be on WikiLeaks and all over the internet. You're going to provide the rich KYC metadata that you painstakingly attached to every transaction.

Meanwhile, we're going to build bitcoin with encrypted, anonymous, private transactions. You'd better rethink this Bubble Boy, this panopticon, because **building resilient systems is about exposing them to continuous attack.** Eating mudcakes is how you build resilient systems.

I'm not scared of permissioned ledgers—denatured, defanged, centralized, weak systems behind bubbles. Those are not going to scale, they're not going to survive, they're not going to be secure, they're not going to provide privacy; but they *are* going to backfire badly.

More Bubbles!

The funny thing is, that lesson is going to take a long time to learn. I can see it now:

"Sir, we had all of the drone assassination things behind a firewall, but someone burst through the bubble."

"All right, call the General. Get me two bubbles, we're going to double up! Bubbles within bubbles."

"Sir, they burst through our double-bubble."

"Titanium bubbles! If we paid Lockheed Martin $100 million, maybe they can build us a double titanium bubble to hide all our data behind?"

"Sir, it lasted 30 seconds before Anonymous ripped it to shreds and threw all of our data on the internet."

"Hmm, I wonder if we can build more bubbles?"

Building the Security Swarm

They think that having your data on the Internet, without controlling it centrally, is weakness. It isn't weakness. That sewer rat out there isn't weak. It's the strongest thing we can build, because it's constantly under attack. Wrapping it in a bubble doesn't make it stronger; it gradually denatures and weakens it until what's left is a pale, immunosuppressed, little lab rat with red eyes that dies the first time it's exposed to the flu.

That's what security is. **Security is a process—a process of openness and exposure. It's a process of continually adapting to new attacks, and in that process, dynamically becoming more and more robust, less and less fragile.**

We're introducing bitcoin in a world full of fragile systems: central banks, centralized banking, monetary systems that can't manage to achieve liftoff in the economy. In that environment, we're introducing a robust, global, decentralized system. It's robust today; it's not perfect, it's got bugs, but we don't hide those bugs —we announce them, we glorify in them, we discuss them, we invite people to attack it. We take that information and we make it stronger every single day.

That is why we win. Because while they're building Bubble Boy, we're building a swarm of sewer rats.

Thank you.

A New Species of Money

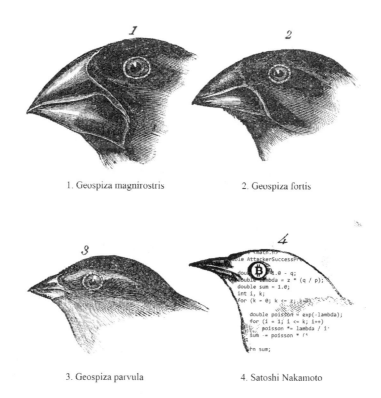

1. Geospiza magnirostris

2. Geospiza fortis

3. Geospiza parvula

4. Satoshi Nakamoto

Bitcoin Milano Meetup; Milano, Italy; May 2016

Video Link: https://youtu.be/G-25w7Zh8zk

A Small Ripple Spreading

Today, I'm going to be talking about money from an evolutionary perspective. This topic is something that I've been thinking about for quite a while. I have a great interest in the subject of evolutionary biology, but I'm not a biologist. There are probably no biologists in the audience, which is a good thing because I will say things that will probably upset biologists, because I'll get them wrong.

I'm speaking in general terms and this is more of a narrative to help you understand where things are going.

Something really important happened on January 3rd, 2009. The world changed. But as with many fundamental and significant changes in the world, very few people noticed. Almost no one noticed. That change started out as a small ripple, and it continued spreading. Now we are here, 7 years later, and that small change, bitcoin, is radically rewriting human history and human society. We are part of something unique. We are part of something really special, something that started as an idea—and even the inventor of the idea wasn't sure it would work. And at first the people who looked at the idea, those who looked at the theory behind bitcoin, had many things to say about how it wouldn't work.

On the internet, some of the most interesting things are things that do not work in theory but *do* work in practice. My favorite example is Wikipedia. If you think about Wikipedia objectively, based on what you know about human nature, it shouldn't work. Why would anyone spend months of their time writing an article about a single Pokémon card for free? That doesn't make any sense, and yet people do that. We underestimate human nature sometimes.

Bitcoin is like that. In theory, it's difficult to understand how it works; in practice, it has spawned a revolution. It has created something very new.

New Money, New Niche

The era before bitcoin can be characterized by a short-lived period of time which started in the beginning of the twentieth century, with the introduction of central banking. For the first time, money became completely detached from commodity and became managed on a national basis by central banks. This was a very different model than we'd had before, and it continues to this day. Many of us in bitcoin believe that, when we look back a hundred years from now, we will see central banking as a short-lived and not particularly successful experiment.

Bitcoin is different, not because it replaces central banking, but because it opens the door to a new form of competition—a form of competition where money can be created on the internet by anyone, and that money can be instantaneously global, unforgeable, open, and secure. With that new system, we not only created a new form of money, but we also created a new environmental niche for money to compete in.

In my opinion, **with the invention of internet money, we are now starting to see the first models of the network-centric evolution of money, where different forms of money compete as species.** They compete by finding an environmental niche and adapting to that niche through simple competition.

This has never happened before. The reason it's never happened before is because the environment was hostile to that form of money. Borders, geography, nation-states limited the ability of money to spread and compete with other money on a global basis. What happened on January 3rd, 2009, was a very significant event because it fundamentally changed the environment in which money competes.

Punctuated Equilibrium

The best similar example I can provide is a reference to a very special moment for the history of this planet, when the levels of oxygen in the atmosphere started rising. That created the possibility of aerobic metabolism, meaning that species could now metabolize with oxygen. Before that, all species were anaerobic: they metabolized without oxygen, they lived in an oxygen-free environment. In fact, for them oxygen is toxic; oxygen is an oxidizer, it's poison to an anaerobic organism. It's like an acid; it destroys them.

What happened when the environment changed to allow aerobic metabolism? Suddenly, a whole new environment opened up for species to compete, species that were not competing with the previous species because they operated in a completely different niche. They had a significant advantage, because aerobic metabolism is an order of magnitude more efficient. Within a very short period of time, the planet changed. Anaerobic organisms got pushed into the deepest crevices of world; they still exist at the bottom of the Mariana Trench, buried in glaciers, inside volcanoes, in places where oxygen doesn't reach. They still exist, they haven't gone away, but this is now a planet of oxygen-breathing organisms. The world changed.

One of the interesting things about evolution is that it doesn't work in a linear fashion. It works through a process that has been called "punctuated equilibrium." Things have equilibrium for a long time, and then suddenly there's a great rush of evolution as a lot of things change. When environments open up, species evolve very rapidly in a short period of time. Then they reach equilibrium again and persist for thousands, hundreds of thousands, or millions of years. Then, again, something changes: some environmental factor, some external stimulus, some advance in evolution; perhaps species are able to create DNA instead of RNA, oxygen in the atmosphere, or (for the dinosaurs) a meteor, or other geological event.

The Meteor for Old Money

On the 3rd of January 2009, a meteor appeared in the sky of our society. Until that time, banks were the kings of this planet. Like giant lumbering dinosaurs, completely dominating for hundreds of millions of years, with complete disregard—even contempt—for the tiny furry mammals that they routinely step on as they walk around the planet. But something has changed and, very soon, those mammals will inherit the earth.

In this new environment, bitcoin doesn't compete against banks, because bitcoin is adapted to a different environmental niche. Bitcoin is not the money of the physical space, it is the money of the internet. Bitcoin is not the money of the nation-state; it is the money of the world. **Bitcoin is not the money of the current generation; it is the money of the generations to come.** It doesn't compete against banking; for bitcoin, banking and borders and physical money are irrelevant. Just like, to mammals, dinosaurs were irrelevant, and to aerobic bacteria, anaerobic bacteria are irrelevant, unless they're suitable as food.

When you look at this environmental niche, you have to realize that it's not just one new species of money, bitcoin, but an explosion in the ecology of money. On January 3rd, 2009, there were 194 currencies. Today, there are more than 3,000 currencies; of those, all but 194 are digital, decentralized, internet moneys. They're the new species that live on the internet. Most of them will go extinct, most of them will disappear, but the species as a whole will continue to evolve.

When you look at the evolution of money in this environment, you have to realize that there are many factors which affect this evolution. One of the factors is us, human beings. We give these things life. This evolution is not evolution by random mutation; it is directed evolution by designers. In this room, there are people who are directing the evolution of these new currencies. In doing so, they're responding to environmental stimuli: supply, demand, the needs of customers, the applications that they have in mind, untapped markets and opportunities into which traditional currencies can't fit. They direct the evolution of these currencies in order to take advantage of these new niches.

But there's also a broader environment, because at the same time that these new currencies are evolving, the old currencies are in crisis. We are now facing an unprecedented currency crisis around the world that is affecting hundreds of currencies and hundreds of countries. It is affecting every central bank. We are in an environment that hasn't existed during the last two hundred years.

When I was growing up and studying some basic macroeconomics, economic orthodoxy said that the lowest you can go with interest rates is zero, and you *never* go there, never go full zero. And yet now 20 different central banks are at zero; not just temporarily, some of them for 8 years, some of them longer. I think the Japanese bank is the longest at zero. Some of them have also gone negative. Never go full negative. Until a couple of years ago, that was unthinkable.

Serving the Majority

Bitcoin is not going to destroy central banks. Bitcoin doesn't give a damn about central banks. Central banks are doing a pretty good job destroying themselves. We live in a world where billions of people have no access to finance, no access to banking, no access to traditional financial instruments. They operate entirely in cash, in a single currency, isolated from the rest of the world. That is an environment in which bitcoin can thrive.

We're not going after the environmental niche of traditional banking because there's a bigger environmental niche. The "gray" economy is more than 60 percent of the economy in the world. **The unbanked, debanked, and underbanked *are* the majority. The disenfranchised, disempowered *are* the majority. That is the niche that bitcoin is tapping into.**

We will continue to serve the needs of people who are not being served today; some of us because that's a matter of principle or ideology, some of us simply because it's a matter of supply and demand, and it is the prudent, sensible, and profitable thing to do.

Evolving Resistance

In this evolution of currencies, we're going to see external stimulus. One of the most important things to keep in mind is that these new currencies *will* be attacked, and they *are* being attacked; with misinformation, propaganda, and in some countries with direct attacks, with legal attacks, with extralegal attacks outside of the judicial system. These new currencies remove power from people and organizations that are accustomed to power. Therefore, they represent a threat.

To whom do they represent a threat? Really, **the question you should ask yourself is: what kind of government and what kind of organization is threatened by the idea of people having independent financial control and empowerment over their own money?** A government that is threatened by that is threatened by the fundamental concepts of the Renaissance, of the Enlightenment, freedom of association, freedom of expression, freedom of speech, freedom of commerce. A government that is offended by freedom is not a government I want to support.

Arguably, most of the governments in the West today are not hostile to bitcoin. They're curious, they don't understand it. They want to see how it can be fit into the status quo. They want to tame it, control it, co-opt it. In other countries, where it represents a more serious threat because it represents freedom, bitcoin is illegal with very heavy penalties.

One important aspect of an evolutionary system is that it doesn't stand still. If you introduce a predator into the environment, then the system evolves to defend itself against the predator. If the predator is an attempt to identify every user of the system, which is antithetical to the evolution of bitcoin and other cryptocurrencies, they will evolve to become stealthier and more anonymous.

If you isolate a cryptocurrency, you trigger a specific type of accelerated evolution. We've seen this happen with species, too. Species that became isolated, for example on the continent of Australia, with fierce competition for very limited resources, evolved to be the world's most venomous, poisonous, and dangerous animals in the world. Everything in Australia is trying to kill you. Australians actually love to remind tourists about this; they even make up species that don't exist just to scare tourists. But why did species in Australia evolve that way? Because they were isolated and pressured. When you isolate and pressure something, it adapts by increasing its stealth, increasing its venom, increasing its resistance.

Bitcoin already has an element of evolution that is quite effective. In the current regulatory system, banks that try to swallow bitcoin get indigestion. It doesn't kill them, but it certainly makes their tummy hurt. Bitcoin can't be adopted, co-opted, or absorbed by the traditional banking system, which is a huge advantage in evolution. It means that we can continue to do our own thing, without worrying about being swallowed by the traditional system. This comes as a huge surprise to traditional banking. Over the past 50 years, they've been accustomed to swallowing any type of competition, and they can't swallow this one—it doesn't taste good.

Ecosystem Diversity and Fragmentation in Cryptocurrency

When we look at the evolution of money, we see this explosion of thousands of new currencies. This will continue. We will have thousands, and then tens of thousands, and then possibly hundreds of thousands of currencies. You think about that, and it doesn't make any sense. If you look at it from the traditional perspectives of money, how can you have hundreds of thousands of currencies? How could they possibly have value?

What happens is fragmentation; they have value, but to a smaller and smaller group, which actually is the normal behavior of money. Money is something that emerges among small groups. The idea of one money for an entire nation is relatively new. If you watch children in kindergarten, they develop their own money, their own culture of money. They trade rubber bands and Pokémon cards and cubes. They use it as a language to express themselves.

Out of the hundreds of thousands of currencies that will evolve in this space, the vast majority will have no "real economic value" outside of the small cohort that uses them. Maybe some of them will represent your most favored football team (which in this city is Milan). In some cities, that's a dangerous question to ask, because half the room says one team and the other half says the other team, and then fist fights break out. Fortunately, this was not a problem here.

You can imagine currencies that represent loyalty to an artist, a sports team, a friend, a business. You can imagine currencies that are used to represent commodities or assets, that represent sharing tokens for a taxi service or represent all kinds of things that we haven't imagined yet. This is a completely new space. Out of these hundreds of thousands of currencies, we will see some that will behave very much like traditional money, in that they will be used as the primary means of exchange and store of value for societies.

Cosmopolitan Currency

But these will not be geographic societies, these will be societies of common purpose. These will be adhocracies and groups that exist on the internet beyond borders, beyond nation-states. We now see the emergence of the first opportunity for the cosmopolitan class and the cosmopolitan-minded people to have a cosmopolitan currency, a currency that belongs to the world—not to a single nation.

We will see these types of things emerge and they do not compete against traditional currencies. We're not going to replace the euro with bitcoin; in fact, that would be a disaster. That would be even worse than the euro, arguably, because the fundamental failing of old money is the imposition of monopoly and centralized control. **The fundamental evolutionary characteristic of the new money is decentralization and choice.** That's why we do not compete for the same environment; we create our *own* environment.

Exiting Traditional Banking and Relics of Old Thinking

When you think of these forms of new electronic money, the instinctive thought at first is to evaluate them in the context of traditional money. How many euros is a bitcoin worth today? Everybody in this room knows the answer to that question. That shows that we are still evaluating bitcoin in the context of traditional money. We are still assuming that if we earn, we will probably earn in traditional currencies; we will convert, we will convert again, and spend in traditional currencies.

With that thought, you have to think about exchange rates and volatility. Well, I'm one of the people who doesn't do that much anymore. There aren't many of us, probably just a few thousand. For the last 3 years, I have been earning income in bitcoin. For the last 2, I have been earning almost entirely in bitcoin.

Gradually, the vast majority of my spending also happens in bitcoin. In many cases, it is priced in traditional currencies, but as time goes by, increasingly it's not. I'm using bitcoin to buy other cryptocurrencies, to buy services, disk space, websites, bandwidth, VPNs, etc. For those, the only thing that matters to me is purchasing power. Gradually, in my mind, bitcoin has started to evolve from a simple means of exchange that I translate into another currency, to a store of value that has its own purchasing power completely independently.

One day, this transition will happen completely for a few people, and then for more people. We will build an economy operated and denominated entirely in digital currencies, entirely on the internet—never exchanging, never touching the traditional banking system. Outside the system. One day, the answer to the question, "How much is one bitcoin worth?" will be "1000 millibits."

The Environmental Niche of Cryptocurrency

You'll have to explain this to your children. They won't have to explain it to their children. They will have to explain paper money to their children, just like I have to explain VHS and fax machines to younger people. I realize how old I am when I get to a traffic stop and want to ask the other person for directions, and I make this roll-down-your-window gesture, and it doesn't mean anything anymore, because we haven't had a car window that opens like that for 25 years. If the person I'm making that motion to is older, they get what I mean, but to a young person it's a mystery. These things are the relics of old thinking.

You don't notice that you are bathed in the relics of old thinking until you have an opportunity to step outside of that context. Bitcoin is giving us that opportunity. Bitcoin is the vehicle by which we step outside of the traditional notions of money, tied to geography and nation, controlled by a central bank, with intermediaries of trust. We step outside of these and we re-evaluate fundamental truths. What does it mean to trust? What does it mean to have authority in a system that is network-centric? What does it mean to express value on a global basis?

As we enter that new context, *we* are evolving as a society. We are now moving into the environmental niche of the cryptocurrency.

Thank you.

What Is Streaming Money?

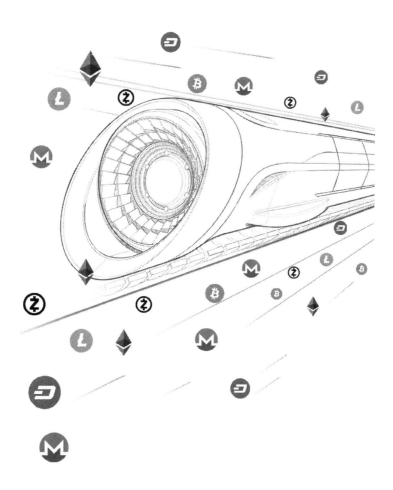

Bitcoin Wednesday Meetup at EYE Film Museum; Amsterdam, The Netherlands; October 2016

Video Link: https://youtu.be/gF_ZQ_eijPs

The Time Dimension of Money

If you're watching bitcoin from the outside, if you're engaged in bitcoin but don't have the time to watch every new technical innovation that is being created with bitcoin, it's hard to see what's happening behind the scenes. What's happening behind the scenes is *a lot* of very interesting work. Bitcoin today is not bitcoin as it was in 2009. It's continuously changing, with new technologies being introduced all the time. The pace in which new technologies are being introduced keeps accelerating.

One of the most fascinating aspects of bitcoin was introduced towards the end of 2015: the addition of a time function to bitcoin transactions. This new invention created the ability to control the timing of when a transaction can be redeemed, when it can be spent. This particular invention is called *CheckLockTimeVerify* (CLTV), which is a very engineering word for something quite powerful.

When you first look at it, you think, *Okay, great. I can put my money in, I can lock it, and I can say this money can't be withdrawn for 90 days.* If some of you have problems with addiction to shopping or a materialist consumption kind of attitude, and you can't save money unless you lock it away, that could be useful. You could use it just like that: just lock my money away for 90 days. The nice thing about the bitcoin network is that when you put a condition such as "lock it away for 90 days," it's locked away for 90 days. There's absolutely nothing anyone can do to undo that particular constraint.

But if you look at this time dimension purely from the perspective of locking an individual amount of money, you're missing the point. What's really interesting about this is that it creates a whole new set of applications that allow us to manage the time dimension of money. This is a game changer, and most people haven't really noticed that things are going to get very interesting, very fast.

One of the first applications that uses CheckLockTimeVerify and CheckSequenceVerify, which are the two time-based constraints, is a technology called *state channels* or *payment channels*. Or, more broadly, *Lightning Network*.

This is a complex technology. Let me start by briefly describing this technology, and then we'll look at something much, much deeper that can happen with this technology. We'll look at what it means to have streaming money.

Bidirectional Payment Channels Explained

Bidirectional payment channels allow you to do transactions between two parties that are not recorded directly on the bitcoin blockchain. Essentially the parties set up a bidirectional payment channel, using a multisignature address, and then exchange promises that have a time dimension.

Let me give you a practical example: let's say we're at a bar that serves drinks and accepts cryptocurrencies for payment—a crypto-bar! And instead of paying per drink, I'd like to start a tab with 10 euros' worth of bitcoin. In order to do that, I put 10 euros' worth of bitcoin in a multisignature address and we set up a payment channel between us. If I buy one drink and the bartender says, "That's 1 euro" (it's a very cheap drink), I'll sign a transaction that says, "Of the 10 euros that we have in a multisignature together, 1 euro is paid to the bar, the other 9 are refunded to me." I give the signed transaction to the bartender, but ask her not to submit it to the network yet—because I'm not done drinking.

Five minutes later, I say, "That was a lovely drink, I'll take another one." I'll create and sign a new transaction; this one will effectively override the previous transaction, which we still haven't broadcast to the network. The new transaction will say, "The bar gets 2 euros (out of the 10) and I get a refund of 8," and I'll ask the bartender to hold onto that transaction, too. While the bartender has two transactions in hand, only one of them pays the bar for two drinks. If the bartender wants to close the tab, she just submits the most recent transaction to the network for processing. But when she does that, I also get my 8 euros in change. So, I'm happy and she's happy. We can both walk away from this transaction anytime we like, and we have effectively transferred the money but none of it is yet recorded on the bitcoin blockchain.

Now, this is a really good night, so I'm going to have another drink. I sign a new transaction that says, "The bar gets 3 euros and I get 7 in change." We keep going back and forth like this until, eventually, I say I want to close the tab. The last transaction we have—let's say it's 5 euros in drinks and 5 euros in refund—is the one that actually gets recorded. In total, we exchanged six valid transactions, but only two get recorded on the bitcoin blockchain—the one to start (funding 10 euro) and the one to end (5 drinks, 5 refund).

Notice that I could have created as many transactions as I wanted, and made them as small as I wanted, because we're not paying a fee for them. We're only paying a fee for the final balance. I could be transmitting very, very small amounts in this payment channel.

Routed Payment Channels

Bidirectional payment channels are a really interesting technology. It gets even more interesting when you combine multiple bidirectional payment channels to create a routed network. Let's say I'm sitting there with my friend, I'm having drinks and he's having drinks, and we have two payment channels to the bar. Right now, I owe 5 euros to the bar and my friend owes 6 euros to the bar. We decide to play a friendly game of billiards against one another and we place a bet, "Whoever wins gets 5 euros."

So, we play a game of pool, and I lose, because I suck at pool. I lose badly. My friend also might be a hustler in pool and hiding this fact; regardless, I lose badly. Now I owe my friend 5 euros. How will I pay my friend?

Well, I could pay directly by starting a new payment channel with my friend. But we both already have channels open with the bar. So, here's another option: I could go to the bartender and say, "Right now, he owes you 6 and I owe you 5. How about you change his tab so that he only owes you 1 and I owe you 10?" Great, so now we don't need to create another payment channel. We create two transactions, one where I pay 10 euros to the bar, and one where my friend's tab is now reduced to 1 euro. We close both payment channels and essentially I've paid my friend, but without having any direct connection to him.

Lighting Network in a Nutshell

Take this idea and now imagine connecting tens of thousands of payment channels together on a network that is routed. Where I can basically go out, discover the network, and say, I want to give Taylor a millibit, which is a thousandth of a bitcoin. Now, I'm not connected to Taylor, but Taylor is connected to Rowan, and Rowan is connected to Jesse, and Jesse is connected to Casey. I *am* connected to Casey, so I will give Casey 1 millibit, but only if Casey gives it to Jesse, only if Jesse gives it to Rowan, and Rowan gives it to Taylor. When Taylor receives the millibit, then Rowan gets paid, Jesse gets paid, and I pay Casey. And that's Lightning Network in a nutshell: it's a series of simple smart contracts.

Smart Contracts Using Bitcoin

These smart contracts use three technologies in bitcoin. One is multisignature technology. Another is timelock: CheckLockTimeVerify and CheckSequenceVerify —mostly CheckSequenceVerify, which is relative time from the previous transaction. And finally a new invention called Hashed Timelock Contracts or HTLC, which is a way to forward a promise that can only be unlocked by a secret. These are smart contracts using bitcoin.

Speed, Trust, and Certainty

Here's where it gets fun. The really interesting thing about this is the speed at which I can process these transactions. These transactions are fully formed bitcoin transactions, guaranteed by the bitcoin network. Any one of the parties can walk away at any time; we don't have to trust each other. We can take the most recent transaction, submit it to the network, and close all the channels anytime we want.

We can now exchange transactions as fast as we can process elliptic-curve signatures, as fast as we can transmit these payments to one another. How fast is that? Milliseconds. We can spend amounts as small as 1 satoshi (eight decimal places, the smallest division of a bitcoin). I now can transmit satoshis in milliseconds, across a network of tens of thousands of participants that are all connected on a layer above bitcoin.

In legal terms, it's an assignment of claims. It's a series of IOUs, a series of forward-looking promises. The thing is, if a party doesn't deliver on their forward promise, then they can't collect on the promise that's coming to them in a routed network. No one can take money without fulfilling the terms of the contact. **It's a system of smart contracts, where you don't need to trust any of the participants.**

In fact, if this is properly implemented, you have no idea who the other participants are. You just say, "I'm paying Alex one-tenth of a bitcoin. Find me a route. Great, it takes 233 hops to get there? I don't care." Just like you have no idea how your TCP packet actually arrived at Google; you don't care. It's the same system.

Onion-Routed Privacy

In fact, it's better, because the first implementation of Lightning Network is based on onion routing, like Tor. Every connection is encrypted. This means that when you receive a Lightning Network promise, you have no idea if the person sending it to you is the person who started the transaction or if it's just someone who is relaying it from someone else. You have no idea if the next person you're sending it to is the end of the transaction or if they're going to relay it somewhere else. You have only one-hop information. **Lightning Network massively increases privacy and anonymity.**

Using It with Other Bitcoin Implementations and Other Coins

You can run Lightning Network on top of Ethereum. You can run Lightning Network on top of any cryptocurrency that enables the three basic primitives:

checking hashes, multisignature contracts, and time-based controls. It's a network that can be overlaid on anything.

I hope everyone now has a basic understanding of Lightning Network. The important thing is that it lets you create bilateral obligations that allow you to stream money at different scales in time, and that it can be layered on top of bitcoin. Let's talk about how that changes things.

The Streamed Experience and the Nature of Pay

Today, the way we think about money is controlled by the containers of money. Each type of container imposes certain restrictions on how that money is used, and we tend to think of money in terms of the containers it comes in, rather than its pure form of transmittable value. But when you change the medium, the container, the message changes. When you change the granularity of time, very strange things start to happen.

How many of you are paid by salary? How many of you receive your salary automatically through your bank account? Okay, that's almost three-quarters of the audience. And how often do you get paid? Once a month? Why?

This is a question we haven't really considered: what is the nature of salary and why does it occur at monthly intervals? Why do we chunk money at monthly intervals? There's a very good reason. This is an example of money acquiring the characteristics of its container. The medium of banking payments, the accounting systems, the ability to pay employees, are constrained. It gets expensive to make transfers more often using the banking system.

Streaming Music, Streaming Movies

Let's look at some parallels in history. Right now, we're living on the internet in the era of streaming. Streaming has become one of these enormously powerful concepts that is changing the way we consume various things, the way we experience various things on the internet. For example, MP3 music is disappearing. Why? Because I don't want to hold 30,000 MP3s on my mobile device when I can stream them in real time from a provider. How many people here have stopped storing MP3s on their mobile devices and use a streaming service? That's 75 percent of the audience. This concept didn't exist 10 years ago.

A lot of us who were involved in the early internet recognized that, at some point, the value of storing the data versus streaming it live would switch and no one would store their own music collection. In fact, now a lot of the value comes from the curation—the DJ, the playlist. If I take the 30,000 MP3s on my laptop, and I hit "shuffle," bad things happen. Why? Because I have a very broad, multigenre music collection. I may go from Tchaikovsky to Iron Maiden to Justin Bieber in 3 minutes. And that may damage my psyche, especially if I end with Justin Bieber (okay, I don't actually own any Justin Bieber, but just as an example). **The bottom line is that we now value not the permanence of music but the experience of music. It's changed how we experience music.**

The same thing happened with video cassettes. Do you remember when you had to go to the store to get a video cassette? For anybody under 30 years old, a video cassette was this plastic thing that you had to rewind; kind of like a DVD, only suckier. If you experience movies that way, it changes your experience. You have a limited catalog and you very carefully consider what you buy. You experience it in a different way; you actually sit down through a whole movie and enjoy it. Now, we have streaming video and we've changed our expectations. It hasn't just changed our expectations in how we acquire movies, like using Netflix. The really important impact is the emergence of things like YouTube. We've gone from experiencing video content in an hour and a half to experiencing video content in 15 minutes, to now experiencing video content in 6-second Vines and insta-videos. That experience is completely different.

You see, when the container changed, the actual experience of video changed. Now you could start experiencing video in much smaller amounts. It could be created by a whole lot of people you've never met, who didn't have any production talent, and still sometimes be surprisingly good. Streaming video changed the nature of video. Streaming music changed the nature of music.

Streaming Money and Cash Flows

What happens when we start streaming money? If we can do payments that are on a millisecond frequency, that are as low as a satoshi, why not get your salary paid every minute? This has some really important implications. If you think about it purely from the perspective of salary, now you're working in real time. **Money becomes a real-time thing and its nature fundamentally changes.**

I watched an interesting video the other day. A team at a university created a camera that could take 1 trillion frames per second. They shined a beam of light through a plastic bottle and recorded it with their camera. In the video, the beam of light suddenly changes into a chunk of light that moves through the bottle. You can actually see photons, individual photons, clumped together as a pulse of light, moving through the bottle. Light is actually quanta, it's discrete units. But in our everyday experience, it's not: it's a wave, it's a flow. Nature is like that.

What happens when you change the time dimension of money? What happens when you convert it from something that is packetized—that is discrete, something that we've been used to dealing with for generations now in chunks of monthly payments and quarterly accounting and (maybe if we're lucky) daily payments— and take it down to milliseconds? When you can do micropayments in milliseconds, the term *cash flow* takes on a whole different meaning. **Cash *is* a flow; it's a continuous stream that has no meaning as an amount.** Imagine doing accounting in businesses on a real-time basis, based on flows of money coming in and flows of money coming out. We have not even scratched the surface. Until now.

Compressing Payments, Changing Systems

Just as the internet converged all media onto a single network, bitcoin and cryptocurrencies converge payment networks. If you were here before the internet (and I certainly was), we had communication networks for sending photos, which we called fax. We had communication networks for sending letters, called telex. We had communication networks for sending voice, and we called that a telephone. The internet brought all of these together.

Today, we have payment networks that are big, for governments to pay each other; payment networks that are small, for us to pay each other; payment networks that are for consumer to business, for retail. Payment networks that are for large amounts, payment networks that are for small amounts.

Bitcoin allows us to do transactions as small as a microtransaction all the way to the level of a gigatransaction. It has compressed the space of payments, so that a single network can support making payments worth billions and making payments worth pennies. That's compressing space. Now, with this introduction of a time dimension into bitcoin, we are going to compress time. **We are going to open up a completely new dimension to money, one that allows us to address money as minute flows that flow continuously, that can be aggregated and split as streams.**

When I say "streaming money," it's going to take 15 years for us to really understand what that means: what that does to human payments, what that does to corporate payments, what that does to cross-border payments, what that does to the nation-state. I don't know what that will be yet, but I do know one thing: it's going to be big. That's what streaming money is.

Thank you.

The Lion and the Shark

Silicon Valley Ethereum Meetup at Institute for the Future; Mountain View, California; September 2016

Video Link: https://youtu.be/d0x6CtD8iq4

Comparing Bitcoin and Ethereum

Some people have called me a "bitcoin maximalist." I am not a bitcoin maximalist. **I am interested in the possibility of open, public, borderless, decentralized, permissionless blockchains, disrupting everything.** In that space, I think there is plenty of room for many different approaches to many different problems.

So what is Ethereum? What is bitcoin? How do the two compare? Let's see what Google has to say. If I type into Google's search bar "Ethereum is…," Google suggests as the first search "Ethereum is… dead." The good news is, Ethereum is not alone in that. If you type "bitcoin is..," Google suggests that "bitcoin is… dead."

Already, we see that **these two systems share one thing in common: they are consistently underestimated. I call them "zombie currencies."** Even after the double tap, as you're walking out of the supermarket you just looted during the zombie apocalypse, you hear "grrr!" behind you. As always, the zombie refuses to die.

If you actually run the search "Ethereum is…," you'll find a definition from the Ethereum.org website: "Ethereum is a decentralized platform that runs smart contracts: applications that run exactly as programmed without any possibility of downtime, censorship, fraud or third party interference." If you type "Bitcoin is…," you'll see the title of Satoshi Nakamoto's white paper that says, "Bitcoin is a system of peer-to-peer electronic cash."

Now we have to ask, are these what they say they are? Is Ethereum, in fact, what it says it is on the website? Is bitcoin what it says it is in the white paper? By asking that question, we have to look at the inescapable conclusion: **what the founder wants something to be is not always what that thing is.**

Unintended Consequences

That shouldn't be surprising, it applies to every technology. The more disruptive it is, the less a founder or inventor is able to predict what it will end up being, how it will evolve, what fitness it will find for what applications.

"The internet is…" a military network designed to allow the continuity of data routing in the case of a targeted, strategic, nuclear attack against the United States.

Or, the world's largest single repository of cat videos. DARPA did not set out to create the world's largest single repository of cat videos.

Tim Berners-Lee designed the web to be a mechanism for physicists to be able to exchange knowledge—papers, data, images—between research institutions, not to post photos of what they just ate, or to use just the right camera angle, with just the right pouty duckface look, to impress everyone in the world simultaneously. Unintended consequences are part of technology.

Choices Are Evolutionary Trade-Offs

Technology is a tool; as a tool, it doesn't exist in a vacuum. It's dropped into a society and society decides how every person uses that tool in a very decentralized manner. **As you use the tool, you change the tool. Your interaction with technology changes its nature. It molds to become what you want it to be.** That is true of centralized technologies; it is 10 times as true of decentralized, open systems, where innovation does not require permission, where the development is guided by consensus.

It is absolutely naive to assume that just because the founder thinks, *this is what it will be*, that's what it will be. **It turns out that Ethereum is not a system of applications that run exactly as written, without third-party interference or censorship, etc. Bitcoin is not simply a system of peer-to-peer digital cash.** Systems evolve, and the tricky thing about evolution is, even when it's directed, when you make a choice on any feature of the system, you're constrained by two things: 1) you have no idea what the marketplace or society will do with that choice, what path it will send you down; and 2) when you make that choice, you are always making a trade-off.

If you choose one path, you close the possibility of pursuing other paths. If you're a shark and you have gills, you can breathe in salt water; but by necessity, you cannot breathe in open air. If you're a lion and you develop claws, you will not have the dexterity of primate fingers. Every choice opens one path and closes billions of other possibilities that could have been pursued. Even if you knew exactly where you're going, choices have consequences. They limit things, they are inherently trade-offs.

Kings of Environmental Niches

I'm using the lion and the shark as an example because I think that it illustrates one way to look at Ethereum and bitcoin, when comparing them. If Ethereum is a shark, it is the apex predator within its own environment. It's a fast swimmer, it can breathe underwater, it eats anything that bothers it. If bitcoin is a lion, it rules the land but it doesn't swim very well. You can never really put these two apex predators in a fighting ring together and say, "Let the best one win!" Because the outcome is decided entirely by whether you fill that ring with water or not.

Fitness for purpose is something that is decided through this evolutionary process, in a marketplace. There is no such thing as "best." In evolutionary terms, fitness does not mean "the strongest"; it means the one that has the best adaptation for its environment.

Then the question becomes: what is the environment for Ethereum? What is the environment for bitcoin? What applications are the ones that are most suited to be solved with something like Ethereum? What applications are the applications most suited to be solved by bitcoin, or any of the other systems out there? Necessarily, some choices have consequences.

Flexible Complexity, Robust Security

I'm not a maximalist because I think maximalism is both counterproductive and hubristic. It assumes that you have, not just control over outcomes, but even the ability to foresee the outcomes in the future. I can't even make predictions about what's going to happen in this industry 3 months out because it changes too fast.

What is Ethereum best suited for? Ethereum has made some very specific trade-offs; these were not accidental, they were very deliberate. It is a Turing-complete language, which offers enormous flexibility in programming and brings Ethereum applications very close to the actual platform.

Bitcoin is not Turing-complete. That's not an accident; it's not Turing-complete for a very specific purpose. It's designed to be extremely limited in its flexibility, in order to deliver very robust security. **Simplicity is a fundamental security practice.** If you choose to do things in a very simple way, to make them very robustly secure, you necessarily close the door on billions of applications that cannot be invented within the limits of robust security.

If you choose to create the flexibility to do those applications, you're also signing up for a much more rapid pace of development but also for much more complexity —which means many more bugs, many more unexpected conditions, many more unpredictable and unintended consequences. One necessitates the other.

Open-Blockchain Maximalist

Ethereum and bitcoin have launched themselves on different paths. **Bitcoin cannot do many of the things that Ethereum does. Ethereum cannot do many of the** things that bitcoin does. **But they can *both* do something miraculous: they can re-order fundamental institutions of society around network-centric systems of organization instead of institutions.** They can create opportunities for innovation without permission, for anyone to construct applications where the minimum required market audience size is two, and that's it.

If I have an app and somebody else wants to run that app, we have a network. On Ethereum or bitcoin, we can run an application. We don't have to ask for anybody's permission. That is a magical thing, it's an amazing thing. What it's doing, in both cases, is creating this exponential explosion of innovation that we've never seen. It's going to affect some societal institutions and structures that have remained unchanged since the beginning of the Industrial Revolution. That is the unique promise.

I am not a bitcoin maximalist. I am not an Ethereum maximalist. I *am* a maximalist for open, borderless, decentralized, permissionless systems that allow us to solve problems in society with technology that is open for everyone. I think that is a magical recipe. It doesn't matter whether you try to solve them in Ethereum or try to solve them in bitcoin, what you think Ethereum is or what you think bitcoin is. You don't get to decide and even Vitalik doesn't get to decide. The market decides.

The Sandbox of Innovation

If you want a system where the founder decides, we already have those and they're called hierarchical institutions; our society is run by them. If you want a system where there is no possibility for evolution into uncharted territory, there is no possibility for change or unintended consequences, then you appoint a dictator who makes all of the choices, and things are much more simple. The outcomes are predictable: economic exclusion, human misery, poverty, loss of freedom. However, some benefit tremendously from these kinds of systems.

But by signing up to play in the sandbox of Ethereum or bitcoin, you are saying, "I don't know what will happen because I'm not in charge." Even better, nobody else knows what will happen because no one is in charge. These systems have been unleashed into a sea of creativity, where the market will decide what applications they think are best. Maybe it will work, maybe it won't.

In the end, these things will fall into a niche where they fit perfectly for a very special set of applications, and we have no idea what these will be. Celebrate the lion, celebrate the shark. They're both kings of their own unique environmental niches.

Thank you.

Rocket Science

Cape Town Ethereum Meetup at Deloitte Greenhouse; Cape Town, South Africa; March 2017

Video Link: https://youtu.be/OWI5-AVndgk

Ethereum's Killer App

What I want to talk about today is the concept of a "killer app," and how we're going to find the killer app for Ethereum. It's a topic that comes up with bitcoin also. One of the most common questions I get asked is, "What is the killer app for Ethereum?"

And "replacing bitcoin" isn't the correct answer, by the way...

The "killer app" is an interesting question. When people look out at the landscape and try to think of all the possible applications that might exist, whether it's in bitcoin or Ethereum, most people try to map out a space to build an application. But those ideas aren't always the first to market, they're not always the first success stories. Some applications require prerequisites, they require infrastructure, or they require a large concentration of users in a specific geography, or they require an industry that has a lot of users all working together to adopt a technology. You don't get the same applications in the beginning of a technology as you do after it matures for a while.

I was around in the early days of the internet and even in the early 1990s everybody knew that video-on-demand was going to be a killer app. It's a no-brainer. In 1993, I watched a live demonstration of a video conference call; it involved two rooms, with equipment costing about £2 million, and required a connection over fibre between the University of London and a university in the United States. It was the culmination of a 2-year project and it was *pretty much* what anyone can do today on a Skype call for free. Even then, video calls were an obvious killer app but the internet wasn't ready to support them at scale. Netflix? That certainly wasn't going to happen any time soon.

When you're thinking about a killer app, it's not simply the set of applications that might be implemented. It's also about what can be implemented with what you have today. What requires the least infrastructure investment? What requires the least density of users and yet provides a viable solution to a real problem?

That's the question that I spend a lot of time thinking about.

Bitcoin's Killer App

In bitcoin, one killer app is fairly obvious. Globally, there are high-value, cross-border payments that are particularly difficult; difficult because there are currency controls, difficult because your government is nuts and they're printing $100 trillion bills, difficult because there are very high fees or low opportunities for banking. That's a sweet spot, right?

The reason it's a sweet spot is because it doesn't take much to be better. You could be slow, and all you have to do is not be as slow as the banks. You could be expensive, and all you have to do is not be as expensive as the banks. And there, you have a viable solution to a real problem. All it takes to adopt that solution is the sender and recipient participating. You don't need massive infrastructure to do that.

Blockchains and Dapps

So what is, in fact, the killer app for Ethereum? In bitcoin, we've gone off the rails and everybody's gone blockchain crazy. "Let them call it 'blockchain,'" says the t-shirt I'm wearing. It's making fun of this idea that anything that used to be a database is now a "blockchain." Suddenly, magically, it acquires these capabilities: immutability, censorship resistance, neutrality, borderless operation, etc., which are not really characteristics of a blockchain. They're characteristics of specific *types* of blockchains. **If you just take a database and shove some hashes in it, that does not an immutable blockchain make! But it does make some good money for consultants.**

What's happening in Ethereum? Everything's a "dapp" (decentralized application). "App" plus "d" equals "dapp." Let's dapp this, dapp that, dapp the next thing. Let's dapp everything! Dapp the world! Which is kind of the same thing as "blockchain." Similarly, it attracts all the wrong kinds of attitudes, the wrong kinds of people. The sharks start circling, saying, "There's money in the water, there are venture capitalists throwing money at stuff they don't understand. We've got a hype term. It's the new Web 2.0, let's run with it! Let's take what we were doing before, slap *blockchain* in front, and now what we're doing is cool. And—most importantly—fundable!" "Let's take what we were doing, slap 'dapp' in front, and what we're doing is now fundable!"

There's a danger there. You're seeing it already. I don't want to be too harsh on the Enterprise Ethereum Alliance, but these are not your friends. The idea that all of these enterprises are going to focus their magnanimous attention on your technology and make it suddenly shine in their enterprise applications... For the most part, what they're interested in is forking the code and creating closed, boring versions of it that they can sell to management.

As long as you're not doing anything disruptive, they're going to ride the Ethereum pony for a while. **But eventually, there's going to be a time when what you do is disruptive and interesting enough that they're going to say the magic words: "We're interested in the technology behind Ethereum (dapps), not Ethereum itself." Sound familiar?** Mark my words, that's going to happen. Unless you don't really do anything interesting. But if you do, that's what's going to happen.

Ethereum's Moonshot, DAO Contracts

What is the essence of Ethereum? To me, it's smart contracts. Where do people usually use contracts? Most contracts I've ever signed and most contracts I've ever written are for business-to-business (B2B) interactions. I've signed some contracts as a consumer, but I use far more contracts through my business. Contracts are what make businesses run.

There's a particularly interesting aspect to that, which is that private commercial contracts between two businesses are not usually subject to regulation. I can choose what jurisdiction I want to operate in; I can choose my choice of law. As long as it is an affair between my corporation and another corporation, it's nobody's business what we write in that contract. That's a wide open space. It doesn't offend regulators. It's just kind of neutral.

There's a particular type of contract that's the most interesting; what's the first contract you should do in *any* business? Articles of organization. It's the "Hey partner, don't screw me over and run away with all the money" contract. It's how you make sure that the people with whom you are forming this association, this venture, this vehicle, are going to behave the way you expect them to behave. That's the first contract.

The corporation itself is a contract. That contract is the most critical contract, because that's the opportunity in which **Ethereum can reinvent what it means to be a corporation in the modern world: the very essence of a corporation, the decentralized autonomous organization, or DAO.** That's the killer app.

It's the space that regulators don't care about, for the most part. It's the space where you have the greatest freedom to invent completely new ways, new systems, for humans to organize on a massive scale. It's Ethereum's moonshot. It's the possibility of taking this to a whole new level, taking it into a moon orbit, if you like.

The Rocket Science of Governance

But going into moon orbit requires rocket science. Writing smart contracts to organize corporations *is* rocket science.

What is the essential understanding of rocket science? It is that, fundamentally, there is very little difference between a rocket and a bomb. In terms of fundamental chemistry, a rocket is a very large exothermic reaction. The difference between a rocket and a bomb is that a rocket is a *controlled* exothermic reaction where all of the output is directed in a very specific direction. Think of that as governance; so it's a bomb with governance. That's the difference. A rocket is what happens when you do governance on explosives.

The problem is that when people see the awesome power of a rocket, most of the time they're really excited by the "big boom" possibility—the explosive side of things. This also applies to smart contracts, because **with a smart contract, money is the fuel and the smart contract is governance.** The rocket science of a smart contract is ensuring that the fuel of money, that is managed by the smart contract, doesn't blow up in your face.

When you're using rocket science to build rockets, it's very disappointing when your neighbor, Stevie, decides to strap a lawn chair to 150,000 kilograms of highly explosive fuel and says, "With my rocket, I shall conquer human spaceflight!" Of course, it's a nightmare for Stevie but it also mars the idea of human spaceflight for others. From that moment on, anyone who is searching for the term "human spaceflight" will go online, and the first result will be a YouTube video of Stevie Boy creating a ginormous crater in his backyard and turning himself into Stevie mist. While Stevie had the kinetic energy captured in 150,000 kilograms of highly explosive fuel, he forgot about the governance.

How to Achieve Moon Orbit

The *governance* is the killer app. It's how you take funds and manage them, how you take the energy of a community and manage it, how you reinvent the corporation. Every time you think about writing a DAO, there's this little siren call that says, "We could raise *a lot* of money with this thing!" Resist that call. The way you achieve the awesomeness of a moon orbit with Ethereum is by very careful, very conservative governance that iterates and matures over a long period of time. That is a killer app. That can change how we do corporations.

But in order to do that, you must make sure not to use too much fuel. If you try to build an Atlas V rocket on day one, you will make a big crater, and you'll keep doing that for as long as you decide that the first step is moon orbit.

Let's not do moon orbit. How about a low Earth orbit? How about getting off the launch pad? How about a horizontal harnessed engine test? That's really the challenge with Ethereum right now, but also the tremendous opportunity. **The killer app is smart contracts that redefine the modern corporation. The DAO, the**

decentralized autonomous organization. But if you search for the DAO, what do you find? "TheDAO" blowing itself up into a giant crater because it had too much fuel in the engine with immature governance.

We need is a lot more work on the maturity of the governance, and for those who do that work, it's going to take 20 years to get the overnight success. But one day that vehicle *is* going to go into a moon orbit.

Thank you.

Frequently Asked Questions

At nearly every event, Andreas invites the audience to ask him questions on anything related to cryptocurrencies. As you might imagine, some of the questions are about the basics, for newcomers, others are highly technical, and still others are focused on political, social, or economic implications. Often, they reflect the current hopes and fears of the audience. Increasingly, however, similar questions are being asked by different audiences around the world.

Below you'll find some of the most frequently asked questions and Andreas's answers to them. As you're reading them, keep in mind that these answers aren't prepared; they're improvisational, crafted on the spot for the audience at the event and reflect Andreas's thoughts at a specific moment in time. Things change quickly in this industry. Some of the references in this section, such as bitcoin's market cap, are outdated the day after the question is answered, but that does not diminish the overall value of the answer.

To find Andreas's latest Q&A videos, visit his website at https://www.antonopoulos.com. Better yet, attend an event and ask a question yourself!

Questions:

1. How is bitcoin's value determined?

2. What are the rules of bitcoin? How are bitcoin transactions different from banking transactions?

3. How much do you have invested in bitcoin? How much should I invest in bitcoin?

4. Who is the inventor of bitcoin? Does it matter?

5. Won't criminals use bitcoin? Will bitcoin be used to buy drugs?

6. Should we collect the identity of everyone who uses bitcoin?

7. What kinds of academic research are happening in the field?

8. Are initial coin offerings (ICOs) a disruptive innovator or a bubble fueling greed?

1. Determining Bitcoin's Value

Singularity University's IPP Conference; Silicon Valley, California; September 2016; Video Link: https://youtu.be/DucvYCX1CVI

Q: What determines the value of bitcoin? How is the buying power established?

The buying power of bitcoin is determined in exactly the same way as the buying power of the euro, British sterling, Japanese yen, or the U.S. dollar is determined: through market forces of supply and demand in international liquid markets that operate around the clock. One of the fundamental differences is that bitcoin trading never ceases; it's been going continuously for 7 years, the network never stops. Every 10 minutes, bitcoin's heart beats and transactions are processed. The exchanges never close. There is no closing price for bitcoin; it is a rolling average. A market capitalization of approximately $12 billion is now traded internationally.

What is $12 billion for a global currency? It's a guppy, swimming in shark-infested waters. Every trader, every whale goes in there and kicks the price around. Right now, the experience of living on bitcoin, which I've been doing for 3 years, is a roller coaster. I've seen shifts of 20 or 30 percent in a day. And yet, if you look at the long-term trend, volume goes up, transactions go up, and the volatility keeps dropping. That's an important trend. Not so important to Americans or Brits, but very important to an Argentinian, Brazilian, or Venezuelan. You don't need to tell them why the separation of state and money is a good idea. They already know. Volatility is relative.

Editor Note: For a more detailed explanation of how bitcoin's value is determined, see the chapter entitled "Fake News, Fake Money".

2. The Rules of Bitcoin

Bloktex Event at Technology Park; Kuala Lumpur, Malaysia; February 2017 Video Links: https://youtu.be/VnQu4uylfOs and https://youtu.be/vtIp0GP4w1E

Q: What are the rules within bitcoin? What distinguishes the rules for transactions in bitcoin from the rules for transactions done through traditional financial institutions?

There is a set of rules within the system, about 30 or 40 rules that the software analyzes. For example, if a transaction says my address is paying your address x amount, a correct or valid transaction is one where

- my address is correctly formatted

- your address is correctly formatted

- the amount described is within 0 to 21 million bitcoin (21 million being the total number of bitcoin that will ever be created)

- I actually have the amount to pay you (if I don't have it, I can't pay it)

- my signature on the transaction is valid

- the transaction has a sufficient fee to pay the network

- and so on

There are lots of these little rules, not just for the transactions but also for the blocks that contain them, and these rules are cumulative.

There are also rules at the programming level. Things like, the first three bits of the version number of the transaction must be *y* unless the timelock on the transaction is set, in which case the version bits should be *n*. There are all of these arcane rules which have to do with analyzing the format of the transaction. But your software does all of that for you; you don't need to worry about it. If you have money, you can send the money via QR code, click-click-done—your software will produce a valid transaction.

The important thing to note is that the software is not asking: are you a good person, are you a bad person, are you on a list of good people or bad people, are you allowed to use this network, when were you born, what's your gender, what's your religion? None of those are in the rules, and that's an important distinction.

Bitcoin runs a certain set of rules and those rules cannot be changed unless everyone agrees—and here "agrees" means that you run the software that expresses the rules that you want. But if you don't do anything different, bitcoin doesn't change. The consensus rules remain the same.

Last week, the U.S. Federal Reserve announced that they are going to raise interest rates. Great, so I know what the interest rate will be next week. But that's all I know. I don't know what the interest rate will be next year, and I don't know anything about the money supply. I know what the issuance rate will be for bitcoin in the year 2140, down to eight decimal points. How? Because I can read the code: issuance is one of the rules of consensus, it's right there in the code. And issuance is one of the rules that's not going to change because, if it does, it's not bitcoin anymore. I can guarantee you that we will never exceed 21 million bitcoin because if you try to change that rule, I will say no, most of the other people in the network will say no, and if you split off you can call your thing "butt-coin" or whatever you like; we'll keep the name bitcoin and keep the old rules.

That is certainty. We have a set of rules, based on mathematics, that allows us to look into the future and know exactly when the issuance of bitcoin will reduce by half in the year 2038. I can tell you which block number, today, because it's based on mathematics. That's what gives us certainty. It's not based on an arbitrary decision by people; it's based on mathematics.

Some people don't like that. Some people want the ability to make political choices, to elect people who make choices for them, and for people to change their minds and make other choices. For them, bitcoin isn't good because bitcoin is inflexible. If you want 24 million coins, sorry but we're not going to do that.

If you want certainty, predictability, hard mathematical rules, bitcoin might be an interesting choice for you. If you don't, then you can choose another digital currency or another system of organization.

Editor Note: For a detailed explanation of 51-percent attacks, how governments might stop or take over bitcoin, and related topics, see the chapter entitled "Immutability and Proof-of-Work".

3. How Much to Invest in Bitcoin

Coinscrum Minicon at Imperial College; London, England; December 2016; Video Link: https://youtu.be/DJtM9mR7cOU

Q: What percentage of your wealth is tied up in bitcoin? What percentage of our wealth should we invest in bitcoin?

The answers to those two questions are very different. What percentage of your wealth should be invested in bitcoin? A percentage of your wealth that is equivalent to your understanding of how the technology works and your ability to absorb the risk it entails. Which for most people is a very small percentage, if any.

To your first question, what percentage of my wealth is in bitcoin? I think using the word "wealth" is a bit of an exaggeration. I did this job for free for 2 years, and I'm still digging out of the debt hole that created, but the small savings I do have is invested 100 percent in bitcoin and other cryptocurrencies. But I'd like to emphasize again, that is *not* a recommendation to invest. Because I haven't invested my money in bitcoin; I've invested my career, my intellectual capacity, my creative energy, my passion, my work in bitcoin—the money is the least of the investment I've made in bitcoin. I could lose all of the money and I still have my work.

You should invest as little of it as you're willing to lose in a very volatile market. That may mean something like 5 quid a week. Some people suggest, and I think it's a good idea, that you invest by taking a vice and turning it into an investment. For example, have two fewer Starbucks coffees or reduce smoking by one pack a week and use that money to buy bitcoin. Then once you have some bitcoin, play around with it, do some transactions, use some wallets. See if you like it.

Of course, your investment percentage depends on the country you're in. I'm talking primarily for this UK audience. If you're in Argentina, any percentage of wealth you put into bitcoin did far better than the Argentinian currency did every year for the past 7 years. Even in the worst years of bitcoin, somehow the Argentinian economy managed to do worse. That applies to Zimbabwe, Venezuela, and a few other countries. If you're experiencing 45-percent inflation with your national currency, then crazy bitcoin volatility seems like a rock-solid investment.

4. Bitcoin's Anonymous Inventor

Blockchain Meetup Berlin; Berlin, Germany; March 2016 Video Link: https://youtu.be/D2lZxl53TLY

Q: What's your opinion why Mr. Nakamoto hasn't explained what bitcoin is for exactly and why do you think he decided not to reveal his identity?

In Greek mythology, there's the story of Prometheus, who had the audacity to steal fire from the gods and give it to man. As punishment for that, he was tied to a rock, where an eagle would eat his liver every day, and then overnight the liver would be regrown so he could be tortured all over again.

Satoshi Nakamoto stole money from the state—not stealing the money itself, but stealing the technology of money and giving it to man directly. If we ever find out who Satoshi Nakamoto is, the most likely result will be that someone will either metaphorically or quite literally tie him to a rock for an eagle to eat his liver out (or her liver, their liver). The day after Nakamoto is found, we will "discover" from the media that this person is a criminal, a terrorist, a Muslim, a lesbian, a vegan, an anarchist, a punk rocker, and biologically related to Justin Bieber. I just enumerated eight of the most horrifying things I can think of… because that's what the media is going to do, right? Probably at the behest of governments.

We've got to realize that Satoshi Nakamoto disappeared just in time. I think it's very wise to recognize that Satoshi Nakamoto is not a deity or a prophet; even though he / she / they created a vision for what bitcoin *could* be, bitcoin is not theirs, and their idea of what bitcoin could be or is, is not divine truth. *We* are bitcoin. Bitcoin will always be "we," not a single person. That's the whole point.

Therefore, it doesn't even matter anymore what Satoshi Nakamoto thought bitcoin is. In fact, Satoshi Nakamoto was mostly, arguably, unsure about whether this would actually work.

The bottom line is that Satoshi Nakamoto can't tell us what bitcoin is, because neither he / she / they nor we yet know what bitcoin will be. We are making history. We have to take responsibility for the fact that we are part of making history; part of making history means that you have no idea what comes next, because it's never come before. You have to make your choices carefully and with a long view into the future. The stewardship of bitcoin has passed to all of us.

What do *you* think bitcoin is?

Here's the other thing that's really important to understand: bitcoin doesn't have to be just one thing. That's the whole point of a platform. It can be that to you, it can be something completely different to me, it could be a different thing for each one of you.

In a system where you don't require permission to be innovative, to be creative, in order to launch an application on the network, all you need to do is create that new application and find someone else who wants to interact with you using that application. The user base of a legitimate application is two. For some applications, one. You don't need to focus-group it or test it. Write a protocol definition, launch it on the network. How many people do you need to run an application on the network? Two at most, and that's enough for that application to be meaningful to use.

Bitcoin is whatever you want it to be. It allows you to express the application of just two people, and that's one of its magical capabilities. If you want to create a financial application on a modern financial system, it has to be something that billions of people will use profitably for the banks, which really means that you can have very few applications. It's important to think about bitcoin as something you own, and I own, and we *all* own.

5. Crime and Bitcoin

The Blockchain.NZ Conference; Auckland, New Zealand; May 2017; Video Link: https://youtu.be/jGmtRA9S7_Y

Q: It's fair to say that crime follows money, leverages money. Any thoughts on how you might perceive the criminal element will start to leverage this?

One thing that's interesting about criminal organizations is that they often are early adopters of technology. They are, because they operate at the nexus of highest risk and highest reward, which makes them seek competitive advantage at a much higher rate than any other organization. Telephones, cars, shoes—I'm sure were all exploited first by criminals. If the police don't have shoes, and you do, you can run away! Automobiles are just the next step in that glorious plan.

Bitcoin is money. By definition, money is something you can use to buy anything. If you can't use it to buy anything, it's not money; it's a voucher, a loyalty card, a gift card, but it's not really money. If it comes with restrictions on how you can use it, it's not money; it has lost the fundamental principle of medium of exchange. So, can you buy drugs with bitcoin? Of course you can. Otherwise, it wouldn't be money.

Yet I bet that it would be *a lot* easier to buy drugs with New Zealand dollars than it is with bitcoin…

Yes, criminals *will* use money. What we need to understand is that the tool is not the crime. The tool has never been the crime. Societies that try to banish the use of hammers because hammers can be used to hit someone over the head or build a Habitat for Humanity home, are going down the wrong path. The truth is that, as human beings, 99.9 percent of us are going to use money to feed our children, to give them healthcare, sanitation, education, to give them a better future. That's what human beings do with money. Just as what we do with the internet is store the world's largest repository of cat videos. Yes, sure, there's some porn there. But in the end, the benefits of technology far outweigh the risks.

I'm not concerned with solving crime through the control of money. When you try to solve crime through the control of money, the very organization you give control of money to *becomes* the criminal, then they become the greatest criminals, and then they use that money to commit genocide—every time in history. The power of money is absolute; absolute power corrupts absolutely.

We need to start thinking about the separation of money and state, and understand that it is just as important as separation of church and state. Money in the control of single governments… maybe here in New Zealand it works well. Great, you have one of the few benevolent governments in the world. The rest are not like that; the rest abuse the power over money to punish their political opponents. They use the bank controls not to stop criminals but to stop their political opposition and competition.

6. Data Collection and Privacy

Barcelona Bitcoin Meetup at Fablab; Barcelona, Spain; March 2016; Video Link: https://youtu.be/rwF7nMWUjBs

Q: What are your thoughts on centralized services in bitcoin requiring personal data for usage?

I think most of my talk was about this, but I'll focus just on the "revealing personal data" part of it. Revealing personal data is not simply a matter of a totalitarian financial surveillance system; it's also a market economy.

We already have a system for micropayments on the internet: if you want to buy any content that is effectively priced less than 5 dollars, the price you pay is a microviolation of your privacy. That is the micropayments system we have on the internet. You give your data to be consumed, analyzed, statistically correlated, so that the messaging you receive is narrower and narrower, more and more conforming to the image of what Facebook *thinks* you want to hear, to what Amazon *thinks* you want to buy, etc. We pay micropayments through microviolations of privacy. Our private data is the price of entry into the microeconomy.

We can do much better than that, because as we develop micropayments on top of network-centric currencies, we can instead pay with currency while retaining all of our privacy. Bitcoin doesn't require you to identify yourself; that is not a bug, that is a feature. In fact, bitcoin makes it very difficult to overlay identity on top of it the way the blockchains the banks want to build do, because that's not secure.

When you concentrate personally identifiable information, you get hacked. We have not yet found a way to secure data; nobody can secure data. Citibank can't secure data, the large internet retailers can't secure data, the NSA can't keep its data in-house. The idea that some bitcoin startup is going to start doing Know-Your-Customer identification and Anti-Money Laundering, collecting all the privately identifiable information, is both ridiculous and disastrous. What will happen is that information will leak and you will lose your privacy once again.

Bitcoin does not do identity, because that's part of the design, and it's actually a very powerful part of the design because it's the foundation of us having privacy. Anonymity is just another human right.

7. The Role of Academic Research

O'Reilly Radar Summit "Bitcoin and the Blockchain"; San Francisco, California; January 2015; Video Link: https://youtu.be/aNPEdXQaMf8w

Q: Do you see a role for academic research?

Yes, absolutely, I see a role for academic research. In fact, there is an online repository of academic papers written for bitcoin. In 2013, I think there were only four or five, and in 2014 there were about 150 papers. I know of dozens of people who are doing their PhDs in bitcoin. As far as I'm concerned, around bitcoin we will not only see academic research in consensus algorithms and distributed computing; I see entirely new scientific disciplines arising out of bitcoin.

Think about it: Today, if you want to do macroeconomics, if you want to study the activities of an economy, the activities of an industry sector or a specific company, you can study those economies on a 6-month, ex post facto, statistical approximation. With a blockchain, you can do computational macroeconomics in real time, on real data. Big-data analytics on the blockchain is an enormous area for study. For the first time, we can do things as humans where we can look at the economic activity of very large populations, in the aggregate and mostly anonymous —which is actually a good protection because you can't easily de-anonymize this data. At the same time, you can gain enormous value.

So yes, academic research in bitcoin is great. Most importantly, not only is it happening, but I expect new scientific disciplines to arise out of this incredible invention.

8. ICOs: the Good and the Bad

Blockchain Professionals, BitcoinSYD, and SYDEthereum Joint Meetup Event at Optiver Asia Pacific; Sydney, Australia; June 2017; Video Link: https://youtu.be/Plu_WX3Gs8E

Q: Are ICOs disruptive, democratic venture capital or bubbles fueling greed?

Do I have to choose? Obviously, both. There is a certain contingent that is looking at ICOs and revealing their very statist, traditional ideas. The SEC, securities law, and restrictions on initial public offerings came out of an initial environment that was a crazy bubble. The slogan at the time was "protecting widows and orphans," I kid you not. But regulations are the old way of dealing with things. This ICO bubble will have negative consequences and people will malinvest, people will lose money, others will run away with the money invested. It's a bit wild out there.

It has still created an opportunity to do something never done before: bridge the big gap between early-stage, organic financing and stock-market public offerings, which is a pretty big gap. In that gap, companies can now fundraise from a completely globalized audience with enormous velocity. That creates a very new environment for fundraising, with spectacular successes and spectacular failures.

What can we do with programmable money that's different, new, decentralized, reimagines funding and escrow structures, with protections driven by crowdsourcing? If the crowd is funding, the crowd should be vetting. We can create escrow structures *within* the programmable money structure.

Banking is not the primary incumbent being disrupted; it is regulators and the institutional, centralized regulatory environment. This is not just saying we don't need banking anymore; it's saying we don't need institutional oversight or central banking. A lot of people don't like that idea. Sounds wild. Yes, it is if you don't invent some new ways of doing things better. And I think we can.

Now, we're seeing a lot of funding. Part of it will create bubbles that will burst and reinflate, burst and reinflate, and each time the bubble will get bigger. In that, people will be burned, lessons will be learned, and people are going to build solutions because it will be profitable to build good decentralized solutions that give us consumer protection. I can't wait to see them!

In the meantime, I will not be investing in 99.999 percent of these ICOs because I don't invest in a minimally viable white paper. Currently, that's the new standard for startups. Peter Todd, a bitcoin core developer, went one step further. He said, "We don't even need a paper. Here's a minimally viable tweet for an ICO: 'This is my BTC address, fund me, you get nothing in return.'" People sent him money!

We're redefining entrepreneurial capitalism, corporations, securities, fundraising, stock markets. We are redefining everything financial and the regulatory system around it. Hang on, it's going to be interesting.

Appendix A. A Message from Andreas

Request for Reviews

Thanks again for reading this book. I hope you enjoyed reading it as much as I enjoyed creating it. If you enjoyed this book, please take a minute to visit the book's page on Amazon or wherever you purchased it and leave a review. This will help the book gain greater visibility in search rankings and reach more people who may be learning about bitcoin for the first time. Your honest feedback also helps me make the next book even better.

Thank You

I want to take this opportunity to formally thank the community for supporting my work. Many of you share this work with friends, family, and colleagues; you attend events in person, sometimes traveling long distances; and those who are able even support me on the Patreon platform. **Without you I could not do this important work, the work I love, and I am forever grateful.**

Thank you.

Appendix B. Want More?

Download a Free Bonus Chapter

If you enjoyed this book and would like to be informed about the next book in the series, get entered into raffles for free copies of books in the series, and keep up with translations and other exciting news, please sign up to The Internet of Money mailing list.

We will not sell or share the list with anyone and will only use it to occasionally send information directly relevant to this book series. As a thank you for signing up, you'll be able to download a FREE bonus chapter that isn't part of any of the other books. The bonus talk is not available for sale, it's available exclusively to mailing list members.

To sign up please scan this:

Or type in this URL:

`theinternetofmoney.info/bonus-chapter-2p`

Or this shorter one:

`http://bit.ly/2hAv4sB`

Volume One Print, Ebook, and Audiobook

This book is the second in a series called *The Internet of Money*. If you enjoyed this book, you might also enjoy Volume One, which is available in print, ebook, and audiobook formats in the U.S., U.K, Europe, Australia, and elsewhere around the world. Volume One is currently being translated into Spanish, Korean, Russian, Vietnamese, and Portuguese, with more translations to come.

Volume One contains some of Andreas's most popular talks including:

Privacy, Identity, Surveillance and Money

> Barcelona Bitcoin Meetup at FabLab; Barcelona, Spain; March 2016;

Dumb Networks, Innovation, and the Festival of the Commons

> O'Reilly Radar Summit at Navy Pier; San Francisco, California; January 2015;

Infrastructure Inversion

> Zurich Bitcoin Meetup; Zurich, Switzerland; March 2016;

Currency as a Language

> Keynote at the Bitcoin Expo 2014; Toronto, Ontario, Canada; April 2014;

Money as a Content Type

> Bitcoin South Conference; Queenstown, New Zealand; November 2014;

Elements of Trust: Unleashing Creativity

> Blockchain Meetup; Berlin, Germany; March 2016;

Scaling Bitcoin

> Bitcoin Meetup at Paralelni Polis; Prague, Czech; March 2016;

And Many More!

Keeping Up with Andreas

Find out more about Andreas, including when he is planning to visit your city, on his website at https://www.antonopoulos.com.

You can also follow him on twitter https://www.twitter.com/aantonop or subscribe to his youtube channel at https://www.youtube.com/aantonop.

And of course, Andreas would not be able to do this work without the financial support of the community through Patreon. Learn more about his work and get early access to videos, participate in a monthly patron-only Q&A session, and get other exclusive content by becoming a patron at https://www.patreon.com/aantonop.

Appendix C. Video Links

Edited Talks

Each of the chapters included in this book are derived from talks delivered by Andreas M. Antonopoulos at conferences and meetups around the world. Most of the talks were delivered to general audiences, yet some were delivered to limited audiences (like students) for a particular purpose.

Andreas is known for engaging with the audience during his presentations, much of the crowd interaction has been cut from the text because so much of it is non-verbal that it doesn't translate well into text. We encourage you to view the original content, if only to get an idea of what it's like to attend one of these events.

All of the videos and many more are available at his website — https://www.antonopoulos.com and on his youtube channel — aantonop. https://www.youtube.com/user/aantonop. For early access to his latest videos become a patron at https://www.patreon.com/aantonop.

Original Content Links

Below you'll find a list of the talks we've included in this text, along with locations, dates, and links to the original content.

Introduction to Bitcoin

> Singularity University's IPP Conference; Silicon Valley, California; September 2016; https://youtu.be/l1si5ZWLgy0

Blockchain vs Bullshit

> Blockchain Africa Conference at the Focus Rooms; Johannesburg, South Africa; March 2017; https://youtu.be/SMEOKDVXlUo

Fake News, Fake Money

> Silicon Valley Bitcoin Meetup at Plug & Play Tech Center; Sunnyvale, California; April 2017; https://youtu.be/i_wOEL6dprg

Immutability and Proof-of-Work, The Planetary-scale Digital Monument

> Silicon Valley Bitcoin Meetup; Sunnyvale, California; September 2016 https://youtu.be/rsLrJp6cLf4

Hard and Soft Promises

> San Francisco Bitcoin Meetup; San Francisco, California; September 2016; https://youtu.be/UJSdMFPjW8c

Currency Wars

Coinscrum Minicon at Imperial College; London, England; December 2016; https://youtu.be/Bu5Mtvy97-4

Bubble Boy and the Sewer Rat

DevCore Workshop at Draper University; San Mateo, California; October 2015; https://youtu.be/810aKcfM__Q

A New Species of Money, An Evolutionary Perspective on Currency

Bitcoin Milano Meetup; Milano, Italy; May 2016; https://youtu.be/G-25w7Zh8zk

What is Streaming Money?

Bitcoin Wednesday Meetup at the Eye Film Museum; Amsterdam, The Netherlands; October 2016; https://youtu.be/gF_ZQ_eijPs

The Lion and the Shark: Divergent Evolution in Cryptocurrency

Silicon Valley Ethereum Meetup at the Institute for the Future; Mountain View, California; September 2016; https://youtu.be/d0x6CtD8iq4

Rocket Science and Ethereum's Killer App

Cape Town Ethereum meetup at Deloitte Greenhouse; Cape Town, South Africa; March 2017; https://youtu.be/OWI5-AVndgk

Frequently Asked Questions

1. How is bitcoin's value determined? https://youtu.be/DucvYCX1CVI

2. How are bitcoin transactions different from banking transactions? What are the rules of bitcoin? https://youtu.be/VnQu4uylfOs and https://youtu.be/vtIp0GP4w1E

3. How much do you have invested in bitcoin? How much should I invest in bitcoin? https://youtu.be/DJtM9mR7cOU

4. Who is the inventor of bitcoin? Why Satoshi's Identity Doesn't Matter. https://youtu.be/D2lZxl53TLY

5. Won't criminals use bitcoin? Will bitcoin be used to buy drugs? https://youtu.be/jGmtRA9S7_Y

6. Should we collect the identity of everyone who uses bitcoin? https://youtu.be/rwF7nMWUjBs

7. What is the role of academic research? https://youtu.be/aNPEdXQaMf8w

8. Are Initial Coin Offerings (ICOs) a disruptive innovator or a bubble fueling greed? https://youtu.be/Plu_WX3Gs8E

Appendix D. Satoshi Gallery Illustrations

Satoshigallery

son of a bit since 2008

Valentina Picozzi is an Italian artist based in London. In early 2012 she fell in love with the ideology behind Bitcoin and in 2015 she founded Satoshi Gallery, an ongoing art project with the aim to spark people's curiosity, open their minds and help them approach cryptocurrencies in an easy way.

Through paintings, photos, illustrations, neon installations, and street art, she describes the history, the philosophy, and the common sense behind the technology that is going to change the world.

All of the illustrations in this book have been provided by Satoshi Gallery.

ART

T-SHIRTS

http://www.satoshigallery.com

twitter: @satoshigallery

instagram: satoshigallery

Index

Symbols
51% attack, 30, 32
51% attack explained, 32

A
academics, 101
adaptation, 84
adoption, 17
    density, 17
AML, 61, 101
applied, 10
arbitrage, 26, 49
as a service, 34
as language, 3, 69
authority, 41
authorityautonomy, 41
autonomy, 5
    social order, 41

B
bail-ins, 47
banking, 6
    competition, 68
    fiduciary, 5
banks, 40, 51, 59
    closed, 23
    dinosaurs, 66
    grief, 60
    intranet, 57
bar tab, 75
bidirectional, 75
bitcoin, 25
    academics, 101
    crime, 99
    defined, 82
    evolution, 74
    exit, 24
    fake money, 25
    inventor, 98
    investing in, 97

issuance, 96
money, 70
processing time, 77
risk premium, 49
rules of, 95
safe-haven, 48
smart contracts, 76
stewardship, 98
the lion, 84
time function, 74
trading, 95
trust platform, 2
value of, 24, 70, 94
volatility, 26, 98
black money, 48
blockchain
    bullshit, 13
    characteristics of, 12, 89
    database, 11
    elements of, 11
    hype, 10
    open, 12, 16, 85
    opportunities, 16
    real estate, 17, 17
    security, 15
    voting, 17
blockchains
    mutable, 35
borderless, 3, 13, 69
bubble
    double-bubble, 61
bullshit, 13
by isolation, 57

C
cash, 47, 52
cash flow, 80
censorship, 13, 42
central banking, 64, 102
changing future, 30
changing past, 30
chaos, 58
    order, 41

115

K

KYC, 61, 101

L

ledger, 42
LIBOR, 15
Lightning network, 74, 76
  primitives, 78
liquidity, 25
loyalty, 5

M

market, 16
market-based, 4
micropayments, 80, 100, 101
microtransaction, 4
mining
  cost, 32
  security, 31
  wasteful, 30
money, 3, 22, 70
  as language, 3, 69
  characteristics of, 26, 78
  competition, 65
  evolution of, 66
  full faith and credit, 23
  heuristic, 22
  network-based, 3
  network-centric, 65
  over IP, 3
  programmable, 4
  streaming, 79
  time dimension, 80
  value, 22, 23
  velocity, 51
multisignature, 76
mutable, 35
  ledger, 42

N

nationalism, 48
native asset, 31

network
  communication, 80
  payment, 80
  routed, 76
network attack, 30, 67
  51% attack, 32
  consensus, 30
  DDos, 59
network-based, 3
network-centric, 65, 85
neutrality, 13
newspapers
  revenue loss, 20

O

of things, 4
open, 12, 16, 85
open source, 14
open system, 59
open systems, 57
opportunities, 16
order, 41
orgy of, 51
outcomes
  predictable, 38
over IP, 3

P

panopticons, 61
parenting, 56
password reuse, 11
patent, 38
payment, 80
payment channels, 74
  bidirectional, 75
payments
  consumer protection, 39
  irreversible, 39
  reversible, 40
peer-to-peer, 47
perimeter, 58
permanence, 42
permissioned ledger, 57, 59

television
    revenue loss, 20
the lion, 84
the shark, 83
thermodynamically-guaranteed, 35
time dimension, 80
time function, 74, 75, 76, 78
timing, 16
tokens, 5, 66, 69
    loyalty, 5
trade-offs, 83
trading, 95
transaction
    illegal, 13
    spam, 13
    valid, 13
transactions
    confidential, 11
transnational, 13
tribalism, 22
trust, 12, 70
    global, 14
    smart contracts, 77
trust platform, 2
truth
    record of, 30
two-factor authentication, 11

U

unbanked, 67
unbanking, 6, 17
unintended consequences, 82

V

valid, 13
value, 22, 23
value of, 24, 68, 70, 94
velocity, 51
venture capital, 102
volatility, 26, 70, 95, 98
voting, 17

W

war, 46
    populations, 50
war on crime, 48
wasteful, 30

Z

zero percent, 67
zombie currencies, 82

79253214R00075

Made in the USA
Lexington, KY
18 January 2018